THE GREAT HOLOCAUST TRIAL

THE GREAT HOLOCAUST TRIAL

Michael A. Hoffman II

INSTITUTE FOR HISTORICAL REVIEW
1985

The Great Holocaust Trial
By Michael A. Hoffman II

Copyright © 1985 by
Michael A. Hoffman II
All Rights Reserved

Second Edition

Institute for Historical Review
Post Office Box 1306
Torrance, California 90505

Manufactured in the
United States of America

ISBN 0-939484-22-6

Habent sua fata libelli
(The fate of the work illustrates its argument)

INTRODUCTION

How is it that a man whose entire reason for being is one of love for his own kind (the root of the word kindness), and who sacrificed a lucrative graphic arts career and advertising business handling six figure accounts and earning a reputation conceded even by his enemies as a master of his art—who sacrificed all of this for love of his people—is libeled as a man of hate?

How is it that a young German immigrant takes on the entire Canadian Establishment in a trial that was supposed to be a walkover for the System's media hoax, and rocks the world with shocking revelations of fraud, cover-up, massive impostures and confessions from the leading Exterminationist academics and "survivors" totally subversive of their bizarre gas chamber cult?

How is it that a nation like Canada, which is supposed to pride itself on its Rationality, respect for free and fair debate and protection of free speech, has sentenced Zundel to 15 months in an Ontario gulag for the "crime" of having published a work of history inconvenient to a racist elite's enshrined orthodoxy?

I hope to elucidate the answers to the preceding in this writing which is a study of the Great Holocaust Trial, a groundwork for an assimilation of the exciting genesis, conduct and aftershock of this Stalinist anomaly, which for almost three months (Jan. 7 to March 25, 1985), thrust forth the tattered and seldom-seen banner of *Veritas* upon a world drunk on Boob-tube "history" and cowed and controlled newspaper "facts."

Even as of this writing, Zundel and the revisionist cause remain a subject of front page attention and comment in Canada. Try as they might to exorcize the phantom of this indefatigable sign of contradiction and stalwart defiance, Zundel and revisionism have had an indelible impact which bodes ill for the inquisitors, whose megalomania instigated what Noam Chomsky called the "disgrace" of arresting and trying a dissident publisher.

Consensus reality is a fragile phenomenon. Its foundation necessarily lies upon mob psychology, not empirical fact, and it is firm in its hegemony only so long as it gives every indication of being all-pervasive and infallible.

For the first time in modern history, the consensus reality most accurately described as Exterminationism, was tested and challenged in a court of law. Granted, the judge was little more than a merchant and a bully, the prosecutor an errand boy with the face of a dead fish that had not yet stiffened, and the jury a group of well-meaning middle-class Canadians. The verdict was guilty and the media, "Holocaust" racketeers and political prostitutes tooted their tin horns for all they were worth in crowing over Zundel's conviction.

But it seemed to this reporter that the horn-toodling was a trifle louder than necessary, even in so ballyhooed a case as this one; the editorials demanding deportation of this "horrible lying creature," more vindictive than called for. The whole ceremony had about it the ring of hollowness and deep insecurity, as if somewhere in the sub-cellar of the collective psyche of Canada—and of the West itself—the memory of the incredible confessions extracted from Friedman, Hilberg and Vrba by the jugular-throat cross examination of defense lawyer Doug Christie, could not be dismissed or laid to rest. Try as they might, the Canadian public and even the media cannot seem to shake the meretricious testimony of the prosecution's witnesses.

Neither do they seem able to explain away the preponderance of destabilizing suppressed facts and information offered by distinguished men of science and medicine who testified for the defense: Dr. William Bryan Lindsey, the chemical research scientist, and Dr. Russell W. Barton, senior attending physician at a major New York hospital; of the other defense witnesses including Auschwitz eyewitness and Dresden holocaust survivor Thies Christophersen.

The roots of revolution are deep in the subconscious of a modern public already sick to death of never-ending "Holocaust" propaganda, with its serio-comic soap opera theatrics, Newspeak buzzwords, sado-masochistic pornography, cry-on-cue melodrama, defamation of the German people and, by extension, the whole of our civilization.

This is all the hoaxers have as an "answer" to the revisionist revelations within the Great Holocaust Trial. This is the only way they can respond to all the radical questions it has raised and the bedrock of previously censored facts it has unearthed. The Zionists can only turn up the volume on their hysterics and run those hideous, self-indicting Hollywood movies over and over and over again.

How pathetic they are, and how doomed to defeat. Slinking away from debate, hiding behind a judge's robes and the scene-flats of tinsel town, the "Holocaust" hoaxers have an inevitable appointment with destiny. The seeds of their denouement were planted by Ernst Christof Friedrich Zundel, son of Swabian lumberjacks and peasants.

He found his vocation in awakening his own Germanic people to the reservoir of nobility and humanity of which they have always been the paradigm of Europe. Refusing to let them acquiesce to the Mark of Cain and the blood libels of an evil communications system, he rallied them in a storm of passion and against all odds, to do battle with a foe as formidable as the process of dissolution itself.

That he is still fighting, unbowed and unbroken, is exemplary of the highest ideals of the West and of the particularization of that Knightly Ideal in the figure of the Lone Prisoner of Spandau, to whom Ernst Zundel has pledged his honor and his life.

On a snowy Sunday, on the eve of his judicial ordeal, Ernst announced to a small circle of friends, "When this trial is over, the 'Holocaust' hoax will be known as 'Before Zundel and After Zundel.' "

The proof of that prophecy lies not only in the head-spinner of Reagan at

Bitburg, but in the renaissance of enthusiasm, solidarity and determination that has arisen among the rapidly-swelling ranks of revisionists world-wide, who are coming out of seclusion to form an unbeatable coalition of *activist* truth-seekers, eager to confront nothing less than the mind-polluters and enslavers of humanity.

Ernst Zundel is for the West what Alexander Solzhenitsyn is for the East: a crusader who, through the power of his underground, dissident press (Samisdat), is helping to turn the tide for humanity.

"How many divisions has the Pope? " asked Stalin with contempt. The Zionists must have asked the same of Zundel in equally mocking tones. History will answer, in the not too distant future, that Zundel's divisions are the words that marched across his printed pages. Their prowess shall unravel a universe of lies.

MICHAEL A. HOFFMAN II
Ithaca, New York

I

GENESIS:
VISION AND WILL

Across these hills, there is a world to be conquered.
The mother of Ernst Zundel.

What fails to kill me only makes me stronger.
Nietzsche.

Ernst Zundel was born five months before the outbreak of the Second World War, in a small town in the Black Forest of Germany, on April 24, 1939. His family had resided continually for 350 years in a stone cottage in the heart of the region which had never been conquered—not even by the Romans—an area known for its indomitable warriors.

His father was a Swabian, descended from a long line of yeoman peasantry and foresters. His mother was a Bavarian whose lineage included writers, lawyers, professors and artists. Ernst was the eldest boy among six children.

His earliest memories were of the absolute horror of war. He was taken from bed at 3 and 4 in the morning to huddle with his mother while British and American aircraft bombed and strafed the neighboring towns. The thunderous pounding of opposing artillery filled his days as his mother would explain ominously, "That's the front getting closer." Only 12 miles away, in Pforzheim, the U.S. Air Force carpet-bombed the civilian populace with incendiary devices. The fire from the sky burned alive well over 10,000 women, children and elderly. Ernst recalls watching the huge conifer trees around his home bending with extreme force toward the locus of the city as oxygen was sucked toward the maelstrom.

While his father was serving as a medic on the Eastern front, his mother fulfilled the same capacity at Pforzheim, ministering to the civilian survivors of the unsung Allied firestorm/holocaust there. These memories of the stupidity and cruelty of war left an indelible mark upon the child. Zundel would later choose Canada as his adopted land, among many that beckoned, because it was one of the few nations without military conscription.

With the German surrender, Zundel's father was a POW at Darmstadt, where he was forced to live in a field, subsisting on dirt and drinking from puddles. He emerged from the torment a broken man in body and spirit and would later seek solace in alcohol, amid a Germany ravaged by Moroccan and Algerian troops of the French occupation.

As a child and young man, Zundel lived the almost medieval life of a self-sufficient peasant boy. His family farmed with the most basic implements which they had fashioned themselves. Together, they created an island of self-sufficiency in a sea of suffering and want, and they survived, with Ernst's resourceful mother maintaining inspiration and discipline, by her example of hard work and self-denial.

At the tender age of 14, but in keeping with the German custom, Zundel was apprenticed to a trade school. Aptitude tests had demonstrated that he was gifted in a number of fields, but the family was too poor to afford the university education their son deserved. Scholarships were unavailable.

Since the lad had shown promise as an artist, he was entered into the training program of a graphic arts institute. In 1956, the 17 year old successfully completed the three year course with honors. Bidding his family good-bye, he moved to Northern Germany, working diligently and sending financial support home to help feed his brothers and sisters.

Soon his appetite for adventure and challenge grew beyond Germany's frontiers and he found the solicitations from the Canadian government for German emigrants, very attractive. In the advertisements, the photos of Canada's mountains and forests reminded him of his own Black Forest district.

Zundel's parents during the war. His father was an *Obergefreiter* medic with the *Wehrmacht* on the Eastern Front. His mother served the same function after the Allied firebombing holocaust against the nearby city of Pforzhiem, in which thousands of German women and children were burned alive.

The Zundel family. Ernst is on the right, with his father.

Shortly after his arrival in Canada at age 19.

Arriving in Montreal and quickly moving on to Toronto in the autumn of 1958, in the middle of an economic depression, struggling to learn English and adjust to foreign situations, the precocious apprentice was hired by a subsidiary of the Simpson-Sears corporation and paid, for that time, the princely sum of $93.00/week for his commercial art endeavors.

He was so proficient that at first his Scottish boss had refused to believe that Zundel's portfolio was actually his own work. The fresh-faced German offered to work for three days for free and prove himself in this manner. The challenge paid off, for his initial salary was far above what even master artisans in other fields were being paid.

With a drive and determination that confirmed his early vocational testing in his homeland, Ernst's attention turned from business to love.

The attractive French woman who entered his language class struck him at once as the woman he would have. Sure enough, he and Janick were wed in October of 1959. They travelled widely in Canada, on frequent trips, before moving to French Quebec, in 1961, where the husband found work on a free-lance basis, learned his third language (French) and Janick raised their first son, Pierre. (In a cross-cultural trade-off, their next son would be named Hans).

Being young, slightly wild and brimming with *joie de vivre*, the couple set off on an extended tour of Europe, alternately reveling in and studying the glory and the beauty of both of their ancestral lands. On his return from the continent, Zundel began the third step in his organic evolution into a conscious human rights activist.

From securing a livelihood and becoming one of Canada's most prolific fine artists, with over 600 works displayed and sold worldwide, to courting and marrying a beautiful woman of his dreams, and drinking to the depths from the eternal springs of Europe, his interest turned toward matters of the spirit. What is the synthesis of spiritual action on the material plane? For Zundel the juncture could be found in politics and ideology. Despite social and economic taboos barring his intended path to one particular personality Ernst was anxious to meet, the successful businessman and artist hurtled these to reach an aging "outlaw" theoretician of the revolutionary French Canadian Right.

Defying the opprobrium that surrounds "losers" in the North America which often confuses morality with victory and winning, Zundel met the famous (or infamous) Adrien Arcand, leader of Canada's evanescent National Socialist Christian Party, the man with the foreboding media tag as "Canada's Hitler."

Coming to Arcand as a skeptic and critic, Zundel left him as an unabashed acolyte. One who would learn, must find a teacher, and more importantly, recognize him as such.

In return, Arcand put the 22 year old German through a rigorous course in political science, disabusing him of the holohoax and transforming the shy kid from the backwoods of Germany into a man burning with the cognition of injustices demanding correction.

"It was a French-Canadian," said Zundel, "who turned me into a German." The aging Arcand saw in Zundel one of those God-given synchronicities the more obtuse call "coincidence." He passed on to the commercial artist not only the benefit of decades of experience in the front-line of the battlefield Zundel came to describe as "scratch and claw politics," but also his extensive network of North American and European contacts.

To his credit, and though under enormous pressure during his heresy trial to do so, Ernst never repudiated his mentor. The fascist-baiting prosecutor sank to new lows, but Zundel held tenaciously to honor Arcand's memory even when he faced years in prison as a result.

How different this is from the dissembling certain right-wing leaders practiced after having picked the brains of an Axis statesman or soldier, used the resulting knowledge to rocket into the spotlight and then—with or without the three crows of the cock—denying him to the world.

But Arcand also taught Zundel the limits of politics: When expediency clashed with values like loyalty, politics had to be sacrificed to standing true. As we shall see, the second guessers and defeatists would later take the German-Canadian to task for his refusal to repudiate Arcand.

Throughout the mid-sixties Zundel experimented with Arcand's ideas. Jettisoning those he felt were no longer contemporary, streamlining others and uniting them with his own intuition, he took Canada by storm in a hurly-burly of attendance at university, writing for German newspapers, organizing mass rallies and speaking to any group who would listen to him.

Recognizing that much of his rural shyness remained, Zundel threw himself into the fray, boldly announcing with flyers and phone calls that he was an anti-communist lecturer who would speak for free before *any* group, Zionist, Marxist, masonic, Ladies Auxiliary Garden Club, anybody.

Surprisingly, the invitations rolled in and riding the frugal Canadian bent toward parsimony, the *gratis* dinner circuit lecturer soon honed his formerly unsophisticated and rough speaking style into polished form. Most men would aspire to go from this humble platform to a provincial level. But not Zundel. He had a world to win, not accommodate. What he did next was to address the entire nation by running for the leadership of Canada's Liberal Party.

This was in the wake of the resignation of Nobel Peace Prize laureate Lester Pearson. Pearson promised to cede the rest of his term as Prime Minister to who-ever proved to be the most popular Liberal Party candidate—a post to be deter-mined by a national convention followed by voting by party members.

Zundel was 27 years old at the time. He would be the first immigrant ever to run for so lofty a post. Just in order to qualify as a candidate, he had to be recognized by at least 55 of the elite of the party. He was unknown, unlettered and not rich. Through will, charm and superior personal organization, many more than the 55 recognized him. Running against multi-millionaires, and mostly government ministers, Zundel utilized the simplest graphic arts informa-tion methods: sandwich boards, posters, armbands and pins, all homemade. Spending $3,500 he ultimately gained recognition not just from the Liberal Party *eminences*, but from millions of Canada's citizens.

Not a citizen himself, and therefore legally unable to accept the Prime Ministership had he won it, Zundel succeeded in obtaining his goal of symbol-cally showing Canada's largely European ethnic immigrants that desire and drive, communications acumen and self-assertion, offered them unlimited possibilities.

Running on a platform of pride and identity long before these things became fashionable for immigrants in Canada, Ernst's trilingual campaign demanded not

Announcing his candidacy for Prime Minister (top) and addressing the nation, in 1967.

only specifics such as an end to petty politics, Zionist domination and high taxes, but the warning that the Anglo bureaucracy had better take notice that "second class" would no longer be the contented status of their European ethnic population.

With a few thousand dollars invested in this first major campaign, Zundel had made his point. In the larger sense he trailblazed a reductionist, shoestring-budgeted operation, ruthlessly stripped of all non-essentials, which would mark all his future campaigns. What other men required hundreds of thousands of dollars to accomplish, the kid from the Black Forest did on a lick and a prayer.

Pierre Trudeau won the contest with a war chest of over $385,000. His administration would mark the decline of a traditional European Canada and usher in an escalated pandering to largely leftist minority pressure groups on the one hand and shadowy plutocrats on the other.

Zundel's new prominence attracted to him the usual parasites and glad-handers. After his major speech before an Ottawa audience of 25,000, which was broadcast across Canada and Europe, the West German ambassador to Canada was eager to shake the young man's hand when he met with him during the convention. The ambassador had assumed that Zundel's meteoric rise would be marked by the inevitable opportunism and insipid distillation of personal ideals. He was wrong.

Moving to congratulate Ernst back stage, the ambassador was met by a clipped, "Go to hell," from Zundel. Many months before, Ernst had contacted this powerful official requesting assistance in preventing anti-German defamation in the Canadian media. The ambassador had ignored him then. Zundel paid him back now.

Zundel has always believed in forming alliances and broad-based coalitions. But devil's pacts with political whores and opportunists were an ultimate liability which he realized would backfire one day. The young German strove for quality in people and himself. That would be enough to build his movement. If if wasn't enough, he reasoned, it didn't deserve to flourish or survive.

After his historic stint as candidate for Canada's highest office, he returned to the university where he deepened his studies and wrote a political column as assistant editor of the student newspaper, as well as for some German papers.

Feeling the incongruity of having worked at the highest level only now to be back again with college students, Ernst sensed that something was lacking. It was the "big picture" he needed to call forth inner resources against a foe who spewed mass hallucination the way other people breathe, and so he committed himself to a world fact-finding tour. Having a caring, dutiful wife, he was able to leave and trek the planet in a world tour that saw him wandering in Europe, the Middle East, Black and White Africa, Asia, Hawaii, the U.S. and the Canadian vastness.

The confirmation of his original vision of a reborn Germanity came to him in the course of his peregrination over half the earth. More than that, he saw in the remnant of the organic life of the native people of the Third World, the realization that his work for a German renaissance, freed from the one-dimensional obsessions and self-hate of Exterminationism, would also benfit humanity as a whole. From his world tour, Zundel experienced the life of thriving humanity, the magnificence of the natural plan, and the sensation that freedom for Germany and European people in general, would not be a source of oppression for people of other nations and races, but quite the reverse.

Zundel saw on his world travels that the Third World too would be destroyed if the destiny of European people continued to be unnaturally sidetracked, suppressed and even extirpated.

Zundel entered the decade of the 1970's with a dream as big as the human imagination and as profound as Walter Darre's echo of the ancient European refrain of Blood and Soil; a people married to the land. Reviled in the Zionist media as a nasty "Nazi" attitude, it is really nothing other than the organic belief of all native and natural people in the First or the Third World.

Without being rooted in the nurturing of the land and loyalty to what the Romans called the *genius loci* (Spirit-of-place) — instead of ruthless exploitation of it as a mere bought and sold spiritless commodity — man is truly rendered lost and mad, simultaneously. Such a man is ripe for fraudulent schemes, mass hallucination and easy pickings by those secret elites who preach universal cosmopolitanism, but privately maintain for themselves only, the precious backbone of every true and successful people's movement.

And thus, Samisdat Publishers Ltd was founded. Its first title was the English translation of *Die Auschwitz Luge* ("The Auschwitz Lie") by a former German agronomist, Thies Christophersen, who had been stationed in Auschwitz for 11 months in 1944. In a simple and straight forward text, Christophersen ripped the mask of righteousness off the Auschwitz "survivor" racket, revealing Auschwitz as a well organized and administered, scrupulously clean and humane facility which experienced a war related period of typhus and other disease epidemics resulting in some Jewish deaths (in the thousands).

Christophersen's courageous testimony would later be confirmed by French professor Robert Faurisson, Jewish researcher Ditlieb Felderer and the 1978 CIA analysis of aerial reconaissance photos of Auschwitz taken in 1944 and 1945 which — despite the report's obscurantist text — give absolutely no evidence of the constant smoke and flame "survivors" insist permeated Auschwitz-Birkenau.

Christophersen's *The Auschwitz Lie*, published by Samisdat, became known in Germany simply as "Auschwitz lie." It is the basis of new Orwellian laws in Germany aimed at jailing witnesses and researchers whose arguments cannot be met in any other civilized ways (such as free debate).

That Zundel would inaugurate his publishing venture with this kind of literary dynamite shows that he was not some profiteer or dilletante. The publication of such a book was unprecedented. By issuing it, Zundel crossed the Rubicon. He was challenging Israel and political Zionism at its radix. He anticipated the hellish reprisals and harrassment. He loved the good life as much as any man, but he loved his own people more. Vindicating them, he felt, was both his duty and his destiny.

If Zundel's chivalry begins to appear somewhat impractical and doomed to defeat, it should be noted that he has always given himself room for tactical maneuvering. He will not sacrifice the eternal for the temporal. But in one of his favorite aphorisms he states that he "will not impale myself on the fixed bayonets of my opponents."

The lethargic 1970's *zeitgeist* was a perfect breeding ground for the Zionist method of "silent treatment" or censoring all news and comment, however newsworthy, about a subject the Thought Police regard as too hot to handle.

Christophersen's book moved on its own momentum among the people who were hungry for every shred of truth they could gather up in an occupied country whose compromised government had made a state religion out of Exterminationism.

But Samisdat sought not only to influence the front lines of Germans suffering the mental genocide of Exterminationist propaganda, but the intelligentsia of North America as well, whose power acted as the engine of the world-wide propaganda lie machine. The "silent treatment" is a major obstacle in the path of revisionism. Many another good man had indeed "impaled himself" on the infuriating vacuum of censorship that so often surrounds revisionist newsmakers and genuine grassroots Populists.

Zundel the advertising man and media manager went into high gear, developing his controversial "Flying Saucer" line of publications. Less imaginative potential allies did not understand the tactic. They felt he should simply try and try and try again to pursue more traditional paths to public recognition. Some of them are still trying.

Hitler's Secret Antarctic Bases, Nazi Super-Weapons and the mystic insights of the Aryan Hindu prophetess Savitri Devi were themes the public – and even their commissars – simply could not ignore. The 1970's witnessed a tidal wave of renewed interest in all things spiritual and Zundel was riding the wave for all it was worth. In countless radio talk shows, he held forth on spaceships, spacecraft, "free energies," electromagnetism, emergent technologies and the occasionally positive contributions those otherwise condemned Germans produced under the Third Reich in these fields.

Periodicals accepted ads for flying saucer books that would have obstinately refused similar space for *The Auschwitz Lie.* "When one door is closed, another will open." By this means, Zundel established a mail order business combining several book titles from revisionist and Fortean fields appealing to a broad base of free thinkers and truth seekers.

In addition to this base, he began his now famous mass mailings. These utilized his next spate of books centering on the ever sensitive subject of Allied war crimes. A book in German by that name was mailed to customers and influential persons in a whopping 45 countries from Hong Kong to La Paz, from Salisbury to Cologne.

In 1977 Zundel began massive mailings of revisionist books and information around the world. At the same time he organized continental speaking tours, symposia and conferences the length and breadth of North America.

The size of his mailings, which were the source of greatest concern to the inquisitors, is mind-boggling. In West Germany alone, he sent truth literature to 2,239 state prosecutors, 300 judges, 400 historians, 6,196 journalists, 3,500 newspapers and *all* radio and TV stations. This was just in West Germany! Zundel also targeted every TV and radio station in the U.S. and Canada (11,000); 10,000 daily and weekly newspapers in the U.S., every American senator and representative and hundreds of professors and politicians.

In Canada, every provincial and federal Member of Parliament, every newspaper and hundreds of judges, lawyers and professors received his literature.

Later, Zundel's critics would accuse him of being the world center of "anti-Holocaust" literature, paying him a left-handed compliment and acknowledging

A youthful Zundel confers with the legendary National Socialist leader, Adrien Arcand.

Zundel (center, seated) during videotaping of one of his pioneering revisionist television productions.

that this one-man dynamo was hard-pressing the richest and most well-oiled communications and persuasion empire in world history.

In 1979 Zundel organized revisionist history conferences in Milwaukee and Chicago featuring Christophersen and the German historian Udo Walendy.

Again, as if by pre-arranged timing with Destiny, Zundel's truth crusade-juggernaut gained momentum as a new political excitement swept the West at the advent of the 1980's. Book sales were booming, mailings were at their highest pitch ever, and Zundelism was perfecting an innovation in activist communications: electronic media.

Starting out with expensive, cumbersome, super 8mm camera and recording equipment, Samisdat quickly graduated to video technology and was the first revisionist group to incorporate this revolutionary format into its operations.

The Zionists will try to ignore books. They will overlook pamphlets. But they cannot afford to ignore the invasion of their formerly exclusive territory. Television has been possibly the greatest weapon, after the thermite and atomic bomb, in the arsenal of the enemies of mankind. No tool has been more expertly used to misguide and pollute the perceptions of humanity than TV.

The power of the TV image has actually supplanted reality in the minds of millions who can no longer distinguish between TV play-acting and life. Actors playing the parts of medical doctors on soap operas receive hundreds of letters requesting advice on diseases and ailments.

Former internees of Auschwitz who, as frightened children, were privy to black humor and wild rumors but actually saw no gassings themselves, watch TV "Holocaust" docudramas and incorporate the graphic imagery on the special effects TV screen into their "memory" of what "transpired" forty years ago. Television has always been the sacred domain of the Zionists.

Before Zundel, right wingers had contented themselves with phoning up the TV station to request two minutes of edited response to a two hour Zionist "hate Germans" fest.

Zundel went straight for the jugular, as ususal. Rather than begging the enemy for "fairness," he set about creating his own network, starting humbly with home video enthusiasts who owned the necessary players.

He also shipped tens of thousands of free audio cassettes with his mass mailings. He pioneered "instant response" xerographic broadsides which eschewed glossy paper and high tech graphics for quick, gutsy and informative "combat" reporting, that let him communicate to thousands *his view* of the story the Zionists had portrayed in their media only the day before.

Zundel's opponents watched his progress with increasing consternation, if not outright horror. Financed by the tiny contributions of his many working class followers, on a budget that wouldn't have kept a "conservative" think-tank in office supplies, the Zundel media-blitzkrieg threatened to shake the "Holocaust" racketeers out of their condominiums and into the light of public exposure and outrage.

The media was the Zionist's domain. They cared not how many survivalists played in the weeds with their guns, sooner or later they could tighten the noose around any free man through poisonous and twisted portrayals in TV and the papers. It was only a matter of time. But Zundelism, with its head-on competition for media turf and the allegiance of the masses, pushed all the panic buttons on the Zionist octopus.

Then came the last straw. His foes had been hoping that Zundel would indict himself by fulfilling the stereotype of the German nationalist as Hollywood "Nutzi." But their protagonist performed a devastating organizational and psychological judo. He gave the world an image — not of the monocled, jack-booted goose-stepper which elements in the Jewish community kept constantly in the public eye — but of the German Romantic, battling a supposedly unbeatable nemesis.

He formed Concerned Parents of German Descent and took the battle to the camp of the enemy.

The resulting tension that should have been relieved in free and fair debate and equal competition in the capitalist-business marketplace (which had always served as the Zionist justification for their monopoly over the communications industry), had nowhere to go.

Ernst saw the potential for more tension. On the one hand he knew that to heal a wound one first has to cauterize it. He would not sucker in for the phony "reconciliation" that disguises a one-sided capitulation — a sort of Faustian bargain in which the Zionist leadership promises not to crank out the standard character assassination and smear — in return for which the accused agrees to refrain from all but token opposition.

Samisdat could not make such a pact. True reconciliation signified the admission of wrong-doing on *both sides.* The great injustice done to Jewish people, in the main, as a result of the "Holocaust" monomania and the fear among gentiles of being tarred with the Anti-Semitism brush, has been a failure to honestly and constructively criticize Jewish excesses; excesses exhibited by all nations of people.

By accepting the racist *herrenvolk* claims of the Zionists, gentiles refrained from criticism. Human nature being what it is, people who are dwelling in a contrived milieu of fawning and flattery, end up as out-of-touch megalomaniacs and paranoids. Hence, reconciliation of the authentic kind can come about only when Zionists also admit wrongdoing.

On paper this seems as simple and obvious as two plus two, but in the impossibly exaggerated and traumatized atmosphere created by "Holocaust" lies and pornography, such a request is tantamount to treason.

Zundel attempted at all costs to appeal to what he termed "Righteous Jews" to understand that in the surreal fantasy ambiance fabricated by endless and hateful atrocity propaganda directed at German-Canadians, merely his attempt to strike a balance would be regarded as "hate-mongering."

Zundel pointed out that the very charge itself revealed the hidden racism endemic to the Zionist side: their pride prevented them from perceiving the hateful stereotyping and racism *against* Germans present in their Extermination movies and articles.

But just as any attempt to decry or expose Israeli bombing holocausts in West Beirut in 1982 are met by charges of "covert Jew hating" (in defiance of the commensurate logic that would then dictate that attempts to dwell on allegations of Nazi atrocities are also symptomatic of anti-gentile hatred), requests from Zundel that the wounds of World War II be healed

At the 1979 California conference of the Institute for Historical Review. (L-R): Dr. Martin Larson, Zundel, John Bennett, president of the Australian Civil Liberties Union, Udo Walendy, Dr. Robert Faurisson, Dr. Peter Peel and Thies Christophersen.

FILMING FORBIDDEN IDEAS

Zundel flanked by Ditlieb Felderer (L) and Eric Thomson during production of *Genocide by Propaganda.*

are met with cries of "Never Again."

This is the hackneyed cover story/justification for the continuation of inflammatory wartime propaganda forty years after the war. In actuality of course, *it is happening again,* to the Lebanese. "Holocaust" propaganda has not only *not* prevented the Israelis from genocide in Beirut and against the Shiites in south Lebanon, it has actually given the Israelis a *license to holocaust.* They know the Jewish-controlled news media will continue to flood the airwaves with forty year-old tales of the Third Reich, even as Israel holocausts Lebanon in 1985. The latter will be ignored while the former is pumped up to new heights of hyperbole.

Into this mine-field stepped Ernst Zundel. In a sensitive and decent open letter to Canada's public officials and its Jewish community he wrote,

> The fact that certain individuals of Jewish background are the paramount producers and purveyors of anti-German hate propaganda, and that persons of German descent are their paramount victims, is a matter of particular concern to the German and Jewish communities. It is therefore incumbent upon the members of the Jewish community to cleanse their premises of anti-German hatemongers and liars, rather than attempting to silence their German and Jewish critics.

Zundel's appeal mostly fell on ears deaf to the nuances existing outside their own media agenda stereotypes. One obstacle was the fact that Zundel's mass mailings also consisted of National Socialist regalia, Hitler speeches and other documents from that era composed of in-context statements by the principals themselves. As a result, Zundel was regarded in some quarters as a clever neo-Nazi front man, using a facade of human rights concerns to secretly advance a Nazi world takeover. (It never ceases to amaze this writer that people who are quick to disparage right wing theories as "conspiracy mongering" have no problem embracing the notion of gigantic neo-Nazi conspiracies lurking everywhere).

But this thinking completely ignores the fact that Jews are among the biggest manufacturers and marketers of Nazi memorabilia. It ignores the fact that it is not Ernst Zundel or revisionists who are responsible for the countless swastika-bedecked book covers, Nazi biographies, Nazi speeches and Nazi videos promoted by Jews. Do Jews have some kind of copyright on German history?

Ernst Zundel:

> Who are the biggest purveyors of Nazi and neo-Nazi literature in Canada? Zionist hypocrites, liars and opportunists have accused Samisdat and Ernst Zundel, but let's take another look. Among others purveying, openly and in volume, "Nazi," "neo-Nazi" and Nazi-related literature is (Toronto's) "The World's Largest Bookstore" (complex) about five minutes walk from the Ontario Parliament. . . Not far from that bookstore is "Sam the Record Man" where one can buy "Nazi Marches and Speeches." It is quite clear that purveying Third-Reich-related material is both profitable and permissable, provided that "the right people" are making the bucks. *Why have Germans no right to*

portray their recent history? Is German history the sole property of Zionist hatemongers . . .? (Emphasis supplied.)

One of the most telling examples of this phenemona cited by Zundel, consists of a large format hardcover book with obvious appeal to "neo-Nazis" or those plainly fascinated by all things military, German or National Socialist. Entitled *Adolf Hitler: Pictures from the Life of the Fuhrer,* it contains an uncensored foreword by Hermann Goering, and unedited texts by Joseph Goebbels, Rudolf Hess, Baldur von Schirach and other top Nazis.

It is packed with beautiful and flattering photographs of Adolf Hitler. If Ernst Zundel published the book it would be condemned because Germans are not only supposed to be exiled from their "evil" fathers and grandfathers who fought communism in World War II, but even from any attempt to communicate their impressions, as Germans, of what transpired.

Instead the book was published in conjunction with Rabbi Julius Rosenthal, "Doctor of Divinity", who wrote the introduction!

Zundel's campaign has almost never been greeted by any attempt to see beyond the cliches, to appreciate new insights from a suffering German who also has a story to tell and a side to offer. The media has gambled so much credibility, as a result of its shameless acquiesence to the stupidies inherent in the "Holocaust" cult, that it dare not budge an inch from its attitude of omniscient autocracy.

When the case is examined dispassionately, with a view toward obtaining an understanding of all perspectives and not just as fuel to feed the latest Zionist agit-prop, Zundel comes across as a complex man of honor who simply refuses to repudiate those aspects of National Socialism he, as a human being, honestly finds admirable. Would he but do otherwise, and things would go much easier for him, even now. But Zundel's quest is for full humanity, not that of the liberal true believer who pretends to be a human person but who amputates into bloody stumps those parts of his heart and mind which even faintly question the "chosen" and their pet dogmas.

Such obeisance, such amputation, is neither a favor to Jews or to one's self.

These human details are of no concern to the propagandists. The details don't fit the hate stereotype, so they are discounted. A thorough reading of Zundel's literature reveals a man anxious to avoid community discord, but cognizant of the need for a revolution in perception and consciousness-raising. As a natural man in the Walter Darre mold, he pursues the process of balancing opposites, what Jung called "individuation."

To strike this balance, he wrote repeatedly to Jewish leaders and groups:

> The Jewish ethnic group is not our opponent and we pose no threat whatsoever to the rights, freedom and dignity of any decent, Righteous Jew . . . I do not see why we of the postwar generations should behave as though we were living in 1939 or 1944. I do not want any of us to go through life bent over and weighed down under the unnecessary burden of hatred and fear. It is unhealthy, both mentally and physically, for Jews as well as Germans, and it is destructive to the community as a whole . . . All I am requesting, on behalf of my own ethnic group, is a

meeting of minds wherein we may strive for clarification of outstanding grievances, fears and animosities, many of which—I am convinced—rest upon very real misunderstandings.

Zundel's appeal, which included an offer to speak before Jewish groups and field their questions, was mailed to hundreds of rabbis and leaders of the Jewish community in Canada.

He was ignored and rebuffed.

Zundel's immediate goal in forming the Concerned Parents of German Descent group, was to combat the effects of movies like "Holocaust," the Gerald Green docudrama produced by NBC television, which marked a turning point, an escalation in the utter mendacity and viciousness of Jewish portrayals of the behavior of the German people in World War II.

Both in its fallacious technical descriptions of alleged gassings and in its psychological profiles of the "monstrous" Germans, this mini-series extravaganza, watched by an estimated audience of 300 million around the world, was the opening round in a new Zionist hate offensive.

Zundel responded not with fancy pamphlets and pretentious declarations but with front line activism in the streets, carrying a picket sign with dozens of blue collar German-Canadians and people of good will sick to death of what Jewish intellectual Dr. Alfred Lilienthal has correctly condemned as "Holocaustomania."

Carrying expertly lettered signs produced by Zundel's commercial art skills, provocatively reading, "Are Jewish Hatemongers Beyond the Law?" and "35 Years of Lies" the demonstrations took place in 1978 and 1979 throughout metropolitan Toronto, in the U.S. and as far away as Europe and South Africa as well. Demonstrators picketed movie theaters, newspapers and West German consulates, the latter having lent their cachet to the movie.

Concerned Parents of German Descent received nation-wide publicity. Perhaps even more importantly, the German-Canadians who actually did the picketing and endured the threats of JDL terrorists, took their first tentative steps toward reclaiming their humanity and self-pride, and were deeply gratified by the experience.

Years of mental cobwebs, intimidation and crippling Zionist assurances that anti-Zionism only signifies Satanism and gas chambers, were blown away. Replacing these were the beginnings of a fearless cadre of men and women, housewives, engineers, plumbers, foresters and technicians, who would march, petition, envelope-stuff, bodyguard, suffer the blows of the JDL, threats to their children, villification and loss of livelihood, to stand up for their heritage, their history and their children.

In West Germany the people were not as fortunate. Open activism like that of the Toronto Zundelists was almost impossible. Just as Thies Christophersen was kidnapped from Belgium and arrested under pretext charges for the real crime of speaking the truth about Auschwitz, other pretexts awaited the activists in Germany.

To buoy the faith of the German people suffering under a Zionist Occupational Government (ZOG), Zundel committed himself to a relentless series of massive mailings of books, flyers and tapes to his beleagured brethren.

So fearful is the Zionist lobby of any kind of truth, so insecure of the house of lies built on a foundation of media tinsel are they, that even mail is a threat to their Leviathan-like media control.

In late 1980 and early 1981, Samisdat sent a Herculean shipment of materials to West Germany, even by its standards.

On March 24, 1981 West German Thought Police kicked down doors and ransacked 2000 homes. International news coverage of the Gestapo-like operation gave prominent mention to the fact that the objective of the raids was to seize "tons of banned neo-Nazi propaganda" smuggled into the country from Canada and the U.S. The main target was Zundel's "Green Book," a dossier on effective political-organizing techniques.

Seized were Samisdat flyers, books and audio cassettes. It was described as the largest crackdown on "neo-Nazis" in West Germany since the end of the war, involving 300 district attorneys, 50 judges and almost 10,000 police-men.

All of Zundel's attempts at dialogue with the Jewish community and fair reporting in the media, were wrecked by the new hysteria fomented by the absurd notion of a thriving neo-Nazi underground in the West German consumer playland.

The day after the raids, sensationalism got the best of the newspapers and Samisdat Publishers and its head were stigmatized as "the world's greatest purveyors of neo-Nazi hate literature." Rhetoric such as this is intended to cut off reasonable exchange of ideas and usher in the sort of lynch-mob atmosphere liberals and Zionists are supposed to traditionally oppose.

How were Zundel's supporters found? The West German government had seized Zundel's postal bank account, using these financial records as the basis for their raids and political espionage, probably at the behest of human bounty hunter and suspected former Nazi collaborator Simon Wiesenthal. Ernst was formally charged for dissemination of "hate propaganda" in West Germany. These charges actually proved to be a boon because in August of 1982 the District Court of Stuttgart ruled that Zundel was completely innocent of the accusations and ordered the state treasury to pay all court costs. This was an important victory.

But while the investigation was still pending and as the newspapers and TV and radio networks whipped up a public frenzy about "hate-monger Zundel" (thereby dehumanizing a man in the name of humanism), one of the ugliest scenes of mob action in the history of Canada occurred.

As Ontario's Attorney General Roy McMurty added fuel to the fire by preemptively ruling Zundel guilty of violating Canada's anti-hate provisions of its criminal code without a trial (except in the media), Sabina Citron, the commissar of the sanctimonious Holocaust Remembrance Association, together with the Toronto Zionist Council, decided that more than legal action might be required to have a chilling effect on a free press in Canada.

In mid-May Jewish pressure groups began instigating the necessary "Ox Bow Incident," by splashing Jewish and secular newspapers with irresponsible ads for an anti-German rally to be held in the Allen Gardens, near Zundel's Carlton St.

home and office. Ostensibly, the participants would hear speeches and return to their neighborhood community groups for peaceful organizing against Samisdat Publishers. This was the cover story in keeping with the degree of tolerance of the Canadian people. The Zionists gauged everything with prudence. Canadians would go as far as indulging the Zionist penchant for an anti-German hate fest and public advocacy of draconian action against anti-Zionist dissidents. Ernst explained why in a 1983 newsletter:

> "The Germans have it coming to them," many people say, "Look how they behave on TV, in the comic books, in *Holocaust*, *The Winds of War*, *Sophie's Choice*, *Hogan's Heroes*, *The Oppermans*, *The Wall*, *Playing for Time*, *Death Ship* and so on." These are indeed the stereotypes most people have about Germans and not only are they untrue, they are hateful misrepresentations of fact which . . . have one purpose: to inflame public sentiment so much that real German men, women and children become the objects of hatred, persecution and bloodlust.

At the time of the Allen Gardens Jewish rally, otherwise fairminded Canadians had been goaded into tolerating expressions of ethnic hatred under opposite auspices. Later, as we know, they would even permit persecution in their name. Eventually we may yet see the day when the pathological fantasies produced in some Zionist's mind and paraded across the 3-D technicolor, Dolby-sound movie screens as "what the Germans really did in WW II" will lead to the murder of a German.

It almost happened May 31, 1981.

After weeks of rabble-rousing in *The Canadian Jewish News* and other periodicals, the rally dawned before a restless throng of 2,000. Mounting the podium, speaker after speaker denounced Ernst Zundel by name and publicly slandered him with impunity. Eventually the speakers did their job and 1,500 of the assembled multitude walked the short distance to the front of Zundelhaus, blocking all traffic and seething with hostility.

The small contingent of police grew nervous as the crowd chanted their "human rights" slogans, such as "Butchers Have No Rights" (a "butcher" is anyone the Zionists don't like. Zundel is a pacifist). Eventually they would actually charge the police lines separating the lynch mob from Samisdat headquarters. For two hours all traffic was halted on one of Toronto's busiest throughfares, Carlton St. The next day the media would criticise Samisdat because several brave supporters had stood in front of the compound's short fence, holding signs defying the hatemongers and exposing them for the grotesque hypocrites that they were. Virtually no media criticism was directed at the mob itself whose actions were clearly illegal. What would have been condemned from the high pulpits of media and academe in ringing tones of self-righteousness had it been a mob of Klansmen or Nazis, is ignored when it is a gaggle of "noble survivors" who riot.

The police had held the crowd back, but after this incident, the contest entered serious realms of threat and terror: a business boycott of Zundel's separate, "Great Ideas" advertising company and commercial art business, blood-curdling telephone threats giving utterance to the vilest threats of pornographic violence and renewed court action.

Zundel's will to resist and to defy was being tested to the maximum. As the summer wore on it became clear that the hysteria was mounting. Samisdat perservered with ever greater mass mailings. The video frontier was penetrated and the psychological Zundel judo was in high gear, taking maximum advantage of the notoriety generated in the national media to push his message across. For it is *a priori* in mass communications, that bad publicity is better than no publicity at all.

This is not to say that Ernst relished being pilloried in the press. Anyone who endured the infuriating smugness, cant and mendacity of the supremely close-minded media, will know of what I speak. It is a psychic and spiritual trial unknown to workaday folk. The latter's rights are still protected from defamation because they do not step on the toes of the powerful. But once one opposes the central fraud of the modern age, the media attempts to inflict the punishment of writing anything they like.

After all, they've become accustomed to doing this to anyone labeled with the modern equivalent of witch, "Nazi,". Zundel:

> Only lifetimes of exposure to anti-German hate propaganda could so desensitize politicians, media representatives and members of the public to the plight of a German ethnic spokesman who has raised his voice in defense of his own people. This poisonous atmosphere of decades of lies and anti-German hate propaganda has done much to prejudice my case with many politicians and representatives of the media. . .The roots of prejudice are deep indeed and they are not always fed by differences in skin color.

Like anyone, Ernst suffered from the character assassination, for he knew this was merely one of many"payments" the System extracts from those who would dare to stand out from the herd and raise their hands in resistance. But there was no reason for him to passively endure these media lies.

So he generated more exposes, more newsletters and cassettes and more truth campaigns. The Zionists had no answer to these, of course, and they had now opened a Pandora's box. Having dropped the silent-treatment tactic against Samisdat, they moved to a new, more desperate phase of mob intimidation and forthcoming legal persecution. Hoping to paralyze Ernst with fear for his safety and business, they also risked the opposite effect. With his own press facilities and electronic media studio he struck back, peeling away at the thick onion skin of Zionist prevarication with eloquence and stinging effectiveness.

The Zionists could not answer. To do so would represent the beginning of a debate, one of the things they fear most. They must have a monopoly control of news and education without which they are like vampires before the noon day sun. With Zundel able to pierce the monopoly as a sensational news maker whom the media could no longer ignore even if they wanted to, the Zionists had to take unfair advantage another way, through their influence in the courts.

In November of 1981, at the insistence of Toronto's stand-in for Lewis Carroll's Red Queen, busybody Sabina Citron managed to coerce the Minister of the Canada Post, Andre Ouellet, into banning Samisdat Publishing Ltd. from sending or receiving any mail whatsoever. Commissar Citron had now transformed Zundel's operation into a real underground "Samisdat" in every sense of the word.

This is the ultimate Zionist argument: when they know they can't win by free and fair debate, point-counterpoint dialogue and other venerable Western methods of Socratic inquiry alien to them, they resort to the gag, the chain, the policeman's bludgeon.

Once again however, as in the West German hate charges, Zundel appealed the Postal Ban, and after a spirited legal battle, Samisdat was exonerated. Even the Canadian Civil Liberties Union defended his right to mail, which under Canadian law could only be denied to those convicted of a crime (and Zundel had never been so convicted).

In December of 1982, to the extreme dismay of the Canadian Jewish Congress which said it was "appalled," the besieged Samisdat Press, under fire by state despots just as its Russian equivalent is in the U.S.S.R., had its mail service completely restored. He had lost business and suffered torment but to a street-fighting revolutionary and dissident publisher of forbidden literature such as Zundel, the labors are anticipated as long and arduous.

Zundel pointed out that now two Western governments, "on two continents, utilizing their full powers of investigation and prosecution, found me absolutely innocent of all Zionist accusations that I have been distributing hate literature."

Citron and Company were back to square one. Their rage knew no bounds. Revisionism, Populism and other grassroots reform movements were rumbling through a discontented Canadian society. Zundel was now a celebrity, a person of prominence. He was getting a hearing and more and more people were wondering why the Zionists were not replying and answering him back with the mountain of fact their "documented" gas chamber folklore was supposed to contain.

Throughout 1983 Zundel consolidated his forces for the battle he could sense ahead. He continued to perform important work in his publishing endeavors but the real excitement was blossoming in his video production studio, where he and a gifted colleague went to work on a series of video tapes demolishing the "holocaust" hoax. Significantly, none of these would be allowed as evidence at the coming show trial.

Foremost among the videos produced at this time was "Genocide By Propaganda" featuring Jewish anti-Zionist dissident Ditlieb Felderer, whose 27 forensic investigations of Auschwitz made him the world authority on the faked exhibits there. Together with Samisdat research editor Eric Thomson, Zundel invaded the previously sacrosanct realm of Zionist control with a mind-opening, professionally produced TV video.

Other TV work included an exploration of the rigged war crimes issue with accused Nazi war criminal Frank Walus, about whom 11 eyewitnesses from Israel swore they saw him kill and maim their friends and relatives. It was later revealed that at the time Walus was supposedly engaged in this war crime, he was doing forced labor on a German farm.

As Zundel pushed ahead on all fronts, the bizarre interface between Canada's police power, its Zionist Jews and the media, came to the fore, centered around the ubiquitous Citron. As best as we can now piece together, Commissar Citron was incensed at Zundel's string of court victories and his failure to in any way be intimidated by the massive financial and political clout of his opposition.

Citron and the semi-official Jewish-Canadian aristocracy she fronted for, clearly saw the proverbial handwriting on the wall. The Zundel juggernaut was too sophisticated, fearless and highly organized to ignore. The silent treatment had failed, media libel, mob riots and legal persecution had all come to nothing. A single German-Canadian "landed immigrant" was defying the power of the Zionist establishment and their stooges. Such an example of success would surely be emulated, sparking grassroots revolt. Samisdat's book and electronic media offensive was also pounding its way into the consciousness of the people. If this kept up, eventually there would be debates, inquiries, renegade professors asking hard questions in class and dissident articles in academic journals. The dam of censorship and repression built on the foundation of the hatreds and wounds of a four-decade-old war that were not allowed to heal, was about to burst. The diluvian waters threatened to sweep the liars and egomaniacs into a drowning sea of their own making.

The Zionist strategy remained the same: supreme confidence in the Anglo/Talmudic court system coupled with naked JDL terror. The holy writ of the sacred hoax and the concomitant hatred of the German people was an edifice they would not abandon. Israel and Zionism were founded upon it.

But if the same old strategy of prosecuting fact-finders subversive of Israeli hegemony was still intact, a new tactic would be incorporated within it. Incredibly enough in a Western nation that makes some attempt at claiming a free and objective press, it was a Canadian Broadcasting Company (CBC) reporter, Steve Peabody, according to court transcripts, who would suggest the new twist on the Sanhedrin's old game.

Peabody had read a copy of Richard Harwood's *Did Six Million Really Die?*, a short introduction to revisionism. Tipped off to the existence of a half dozen errors in the text (a good showing compared to the dozens of errors in Hilberg's 1967 *The Destruction of European Jewry*), Peabody approached Citron with an idea: bring charges against Zundel under Canada's obscure "blue law," the "False News" section of the criminal code.

This was a big step, even for the *chutzpah*-laden Citron. The law, section 177 of the Criminal Code reads: anyone who willfully publishes "a statement, tale or news that he knows is false and that causes or is likely to cause injury or mischief to public interest" is subject to two years imprisonment.

Originally drawn up to prevent rumor-mongers from stirring up panic, and which would be illegal under the U.S. Constitution, the vulnerability of prosecuting Zundel under this section lies in the phrase "knows to be false." Mind-reading is a difficult feat even for "Her Majesty" the Queen.

But with very little alternative, other than to treat Zundel as a human being who has some good points and some bad, some things to say necessary to striking a balance and perhaps some rather peculiar comments, the human path

One of Samisdat's numerous contingents protesting the denial of human rights for German descendants victimized by racist stereotypes in the media.

Zundel's articulate exposure of media acquiescence to "Holocaust" mendacity punctured the curtain of silence imposed upon historical revisionists. Unable to counter this truth campaign in free and fair debate, the Exterminationists had no alternative but to jail Zundel and gag him, in order to maintain their hegemony.

Zundel with stacks of Dr. Arthur Butz's *The Hoax of the 20th Century.*

Zundel sent thousands of copies to Canada's school teachers. 25 copies were seized from Prof. Gary Botting and pulped by the Royal Canadian Mounted Police. Dr. Butz's history book, as of this writing, is subject to seizure by Canada's customs and postal authorities.

was brushed aside for the Soviet method, which Khazar Bolsheviks had perfected under Lenin and Stalin.

One occurrence which did embolden Citron and the gang and should be weighed into consideration, was the revocation of Ernst's passport by the West German government in the previous January. It would appear that this was a necessary pre-requisite to the serious Canadian prosecution of the publisher. For without some punitive move on the part of West Germany, Zundel's record was spotless, having been cleared of all "hate" charges in the Stuttgart court and before the Canadian Postal ministry.

Occasionally this writer confronts those who condemn revisionism because "the West Germans don't tolerate it," as if the current crew of opportunists, whores and nincompoops ruling the Federal Republic of Germany from the barrel of U.S. Occupation troop's guns, are somehow the legitimate and rightful spokesmen of the German people. They forget that the Communists and Zionists won the war and have imposed their political, military, academic and journalistic world-view on the colonized Germans ever since.

A good indication of this is the letter of E. Koch, General Consul for West Germany, of March 1983, dismissing Zundel's appeal of his passport revocation.

The leader of Samisdat became a man without a country unable to travel anywhere in the world except West Germany (and internal exile there), not because he committed any criminal deed. Wrote Koch: "Although it is correct that the Stuttgart District Court has dropped all charges brought against you by the State Prosecutor of Stuttgart and that there is no verdict against you any-where in Germany, *this is unimportant*."(My emphasis).

Let's see what *is* important grounds for revoking a passport in West Germany. Koch:

> You deny that the National Socialist regime committed genocide against the Jews of Europe in World War II, approximately six million of whom fell victim. You further claim that this lie serves international Zionism as an excuse to blackmail Germany for money.

There in the open is Zundel's real crime. The West German Consul General goes on to list all of the "evil" activities of the Zundelists:

> In 1978-79, a small group of followers had, under your leadership, under the name of "Concerned Parents of German Descent," demon-strated in North America and Germany, carrying English-language signs protesting the television program "Holocaust." Such demonstra-tions occurred, among other places, outside the German consulate and in front of newspaper, radio and TV establishments . . . These demon-strations found loud and frequent echoes in the mass media. In this way you made two speaking appearances on Canada's national TV network during the evening news broadcasts . . . you, through your behavior, have damaged the reputation and the image of the Federal Republic of Germany.

And there we have it, in the mirror world of the Zionist puppets who supposedly represent the will of the German people, to defend the German people against the shameless lies, exaggerations and hate propaganda of the Zionists, "damages the reputation and the image of the Federal Republic of Germany." In other words, the reputation of West Germany is founded upon its ability to maintain the power and influence of Zionist Extermination folklore. Their "image" would be damaged by the Jewish-controlled media were the Zundelists successful in sparking redressment. Fighting for truth for German people therefore becomes a crime by this perverted rationale. Is this democracy?

With the rear-guard action by the treacherous West German rulers, the Zionists were emboldened to press ahead with their third attempt at legal persecution. This time the prize would be a potential two years in prison for fact-finder Zundel and his eventual deportation to the Zionist colony of West Germany.

In November of 1983, Citron agreed to appear on Toronto's call-in TV program, the Cherington Show, "debating" Ernst Zundel. How is it that the imperial Mrs. Citron managed to violate the de facto debate ban that is the universal policy of the Zionists?

It seems that she decided it wasn't really a debate because she refused to speak to Zundel directly, tendering her replies and challenges to the program host and referring to the Samisdat founder as "this person."

Anyone watching the videotape of this fascinating encounter, who has a modicum of objectivity, will see why it's necessary for the Zionists to *prosecute* their dissident rivals for the hearts and minds of the people of the West.

In point after blistering point, Zundel stripped Citron of her false allegations. For example, Citron insisted that Zundel had been found guilty in Germany. Zundel challenged the moderator to phone German Consul Koch in the middle of the program. Koch confirmed, on-the-air, that while his passport had been revoked, Zundel had never been convicted of anything and he had indeed been cleared of all "hate" charges.

Next, Commissar Citron resorted to the ancient "Big Lie" accusation, which has gotten as creaky as a spook-house door. Zundel had anticipated this and had brought part of *Mein Kampf* into court and quoted verbatim Hitler's words which actually state that this "Big Lie" technique is the method of the Zionist establishment and nowhere advocates this policy himself; score another one for Zundel.

Together with his post-trial, national American TV Polemic with syndicated columnists Robert Novak and Tom Braden (also available on videotape), these are Zundel's highpoint debates.

He remains calm, confident, even relaxed, watching for opportunities to inject wit backed by rapid-fire facts and references even in the heat of the battle, when every monstrous accusation is tossed about. It is Zundel's opponents who emerge as the raving, ranting crackpots in these encounters. He comes off as a sane skeptic and free thinker; not a Hitler clone or goosestepper, just a man who takes the best of both worlds, who is unwilling to intellectually castrate himself by pretending that there was nothing good or noble in National Socialism or nothing evil or negative in Zionism. This is the sort of individuality that marks a fully human person.

Zundel, the European who refused to take Canadian citizenship, is more

"Canadian" than the old school English. Continuing to debate an upstream swimmer like this chap, after Citron's defeat, would win troops for revisionism. So the Zionist's chose the coward's way out. "If we can't win in free and fair debate," they reasoned, "we'll win in the masonic courts of H.R.M."

At the conclusion of the Cherington exchange, the host referred obliquely to an upcoming "trial" of Samisdat's president. This was the first that Ernst had heard of this. A few short days later he was indicted under the Orwellian and despicable "disseminating false news" charge.

From the time Zundel founded his operation in 1959, hundreds of nationalist organizations had come into existence, made an attempt at influencing the public, and then faded from the scene. Some were destroyed by their own incompetence and refusal to see that new methods and new communication technologies were vital to any renaissance of peoples.

Others were crushed because of their proclivity for falling into police sucker traps, executing buffoonish James Bond derring-do and engaging in futile and fruitless violence which harmed innocents, landed the perpetrators in jail and drained resources that should have gone for informational offensives, but which went instead into the pockets of lawyers and bail bondsmen.

Several of the leaders of these groups had dismissed Samisdat as eccentric and absurd, of no significant threat to the enemies of peace and authentic nationhood. Zundel was said to be overly obsessed with Exterminationism.

Yet, who did the Establishment target for total destruction? The other groups, with a few exceptions, were either ignored or conducted their own trials in obscurity, gaining no important publicity or image-building. It was upon the operations of Samisdat that the Zionists concentrated their attacks. As Ernst stated in a 1984 bulletin:

> We have endured Zionist demonstrations, thousands strong. We have confronted their howling, spitting mobs and we have broken their ranks. We have seen our postal rights revoked and we won them back. We have suffered the unlawful seizure of our bank accounts and we have regained them lawfully. We have suffered illegal boycotts. We have continued to put our message of truth into the hands of those eager for knowledge, despite the banning, seizure or burning of our books, newsletters, audio and video tapes. We have continued to receive the unflinching loyalty of supporters who have been incarcerated, deported and deprived of income through Zionist instigation. We have "won friends and influenced people" despite an incessant and on-going campaign of villification against us in the world media and in the legislatures of Canada and West Germany.

Zundel was charged on Nov. 18 on the "private complaint" of the Holocaust Remembrance Association. It would later be taken over by the state. As Zundel prepared an elaborate defense organization including teams of researchers, witnesses, security and support personnel, the Canadian Establishment had a few surprises in store for him in the form of a series of inconsequential court-house appearances.

The legal braintrust of the government arranged to have Zundel arrive at the Old Courthouse for a series of trivial and frankly meaningless court hearings which were almost over before they began. What was the point?

When Zundel appeared for his Dec. 28, 1983 hearing, he was met by a vicious crowd of Jewish rioters led by the terrorist JDL.

In a 1979 California state attorney general's report on political terrorism, this group was described as "an alarming phenomenon" whose members "appear armed and ready for violence." The attorney general wrote that the JDL "attacks with bombs and explosive devices on foreign consulates" and predicts that "the group's violent activities will not diminish." According to the U.S. Federal Bureau of Investigation's Terrorist Research Branch, the JDL were responsible for a total of 15 acts of terrorism between 1981 and 1983, which killed one person and left seven injured.

These facts are almost never referred to by the media who usually describe the JDL as "militant defenders of synagogues against vandals" and so forth. Accusations of terrorism and hate-mongering are special categories the media has reserved mostly for Arabs and Germans as part of the indoctrination campaign which has worked very well. People in the West have a difficult time even imagining Jews as terrorists or war criminals, even though the record of genocide against Russian and East European Christians and the Palestinians and Lebanese is overwhelming. But if that record is not touted on TV and in newspapers it simply does not register in the minds of the masses. They're too busy accusing Zundel of being another Goebbels to spot the genuine manipulators hiding behind a liberal news media front.

As Zundel attempted to get into the courthouse on that fateful Dec. 28th, he was beaten and knocked down by the JDL stormtroops. A small circle of friends who accompanied him were also beaten, spat upon and slapped around by the Zionist thugs.

Zundel rose once again to his feet and climbed the courthouse steps with almost no police protection. Outnumbered and possibly about to be beaten unconscious, he raised his hand in a salute to show the press, the Jew stormtroops and most especially his hard-pressed friends, that he was no armchair executive, but a man for all seasons: writer and leader of men.

So inadequate was police protection that the shrieking, blood-lusting mob even entered the courthouse to continue to "bravely" beat the dissident publisher and his little circle of friends.

Though no one heard Rossini's William Tell Overture, it was as if that stirring European music of rescue and heroism was playing, when Don Andrews and the men of Canada's National Party appeared out of nowhere to put a halt to this shameless debacle in a supposed Canadian hall of "justice" and "law." Though the Zionists still outnumbered the Zundelists even with the reinforcement of Andrews' guys, they backed off. The Nationalists stared them down ready for anything, but the JDL thugs decided to retreat.

When Ernst finally got into court with his understandably shaken female attorney, the Crown announced they were not prepared yet and the whole thing lasted ten minutes. It was then that it dawned on Samisdat's president that this legal ritual was a ruse, that certain politicians had subjected Zundel and his lady attorney to running the JDL gauntlet, to letting the mindless mob

Jewish "Defense" League (JDL) activists brandishing canes prior to their riot on the steps of Toronto's Old City Hall, February 6, 1984.

Zundel (off-camera) is punched and slapped by a JDL activist (L) as Zundel's aide, Juergen Neumann (center) enters the fray to prevent further injury to the dissident publisher.

have its way with the heretic, to intimidate not only his supporters, but also his professional legal help.

But "Zundel judo" prevailed again. By remaining calm and limiting reaction to the JDL to defense only, Zundel came across to the Canadian public as a victim terrorized because he dared to reject consensus "reality." The JDL mob had acted like a cast of "extras from a movie about the crucifixion of Christ." This emerged in the media coverage in spite of the fact that the media always tried to portray the unprovoked outrages by the JDL as a "mutual fight" wherein "both sides traded taunts and insults."

Here again we run into the sort of media "plastic bubble" that cannot see reality outside of handicapped categories imposed by exposure to relentless hate propaganda. No matter what the JDL did they were never referred to in the media as a gang of stormtroopers, vigilantes or terrorists.

One can imagine what the coverage would have been if a band of Nazis assaulted Jewish abortionist Henry Morgenthaler and his attorney at Morgenthaler's trial. There would have been no attempt at equating the acts of defense by Morgenthaler's security guards with the actions of Nazis present solely to beat him.

It is selective indignation which is the scourge of human rights and it is for this reason that Zionist terrorists can multiply their attacks under cover of "Never Again." But "Never Again" ought to be a slogan that applies to everybody, including victims who turn into executioners thereby creating new victims and escalating an endless cycle of vendetta and hate. Those who view "Holocaust," "terrorist" and "Never Again" solely in proprietary categories copyrighted exclusively according to the linguistic totalitarianism of Zionism, compound rather than alleviate world suffering.

Between the December hearing and the next one slated for Jan. 16 of Orwell's fated year, the JDL began illegal round-the-clock harrassment of Zundel's headquarters/home. Delivery people and customers had to walk through a line of foul-mouthed, hate-spewing chosen ones. At three in the morning, the JDL chanted how they would murder, maim and rape the Zundelists inside. Phone calls threatening similar things jammed the lines of Samisdat. The JDL termed it "surveillance" and as pompous politicians and media pundits were denouncing "that horrid hater Zundel," the JDL beseiged his home with an unending flood of hate, even as, in the media, they were depicted as "concerned Jews" exercising their "indignation."

As January 16 approached, Ernst had to face the sad fact that he or one of his supporters might actually be killed or maimed going to court. It appeared that the Canadian political establishment was deliberately understaffing the courthouse security, making no arrests of the JDL terrorists and generally creating an atmosphere conducive to a lynching.

This comes as no surprise to students of the psychological warfare principles imbedded in "Holocaust" movies. The lingering and graphic acting out of Jewish fantasies about what Germans supposedly did, gives the public a latter-day witch to punish, hang and burn. Remember, the slogan of the JDL is "Butchers have no rights" – and it is the JDL who will decide what the definition of butcher is.

Hence we see that *in the name of allegedly combatting hate, hateful tactics are openly employed with the acquiesence of the authorities; in the name of defending human rights, one segment of humanity* (the JDL-identified "butchers") is said to have no rights.

Ernst decided to defend himself with a rigorously disciplined corps of supporters. He well recognized what one *agent-provocateur*, one misspoken word of anger, one Viking-type warrior fed up with the spittle in his face, might cost Samisdat. The Jews could commit any outrage, shout any insult about the German people, beat and pummel anybody and because they were stereotyped by a thousand movies as victims and martyrs their actions would be completely overlooked. But let one Zundelist break ranks or abandon discipline and cries of "Nazi baby-killers" would be heard across Canada. The discipline of the Zundelists was a key to their success.

His other option was simply to repeat the pacifist December appearance, where he and a few friends threw themselves on the mercy of the police. Now, Ernst chose self-defense. Part of his attitude was one of defiant upholding of basic rights for anti-Zionists. This was something misunderstood at first by his potential allies among the Populist and Revisionist movements. They had equated his prudence, strategy, troop-discipline and caution with cowardice and inaction.

Ernst would fight to defend himself both physically and intellectually. He had not wanted it this way. The fact that it had come this far shattered his dream of reconciliation with honest Jewish leaders pioneering a new world based on admissions from both sides. That dream lay on the garbage heap of history. Now his first goal had to be survival and to do that he had to show the world that one can defy the supposedly "divine," "almighty" Zionists and live to tell about it.

Issuing his men yellow plastic hard hats for crucial protection of the head, selecting a trained medic with a clearly marked Red Cross and carefully screening all security personnel, he was about to put together a disciplined unit that would be cool under fire but which would accomplish their objective of getting Zundel and his attorney safely into court, simultaneously shaming the politicians who held the police back and encouraged a potential riot, or worse. Zundel:

> On Jan. 16, 1984, in the fateful year of George Orwell, I once again approached the courthouse steps to find an even larger and certainly more violent mob of Zionist thugs who attempted to bar my way into court. By this time I had reinforcements, as several more of my friends had volunteered to assist me in entering the courtroom. *We literally fought our way up the steps and into the courthouse* . . . Once again, the authorities had seen fit to stock the courthouse precincts with only a token number of policemen, several of whom were knocked down or struck by Zionist demonstrators themselves. *Even elderly people who accompanied us into the courthouse were attacked without mercy and knocked to the ground.*

Samisdat researcher Eric Thomson was slammed to the ground by JDL attackers. He was kicked repeatedly by a Jewess, his glasses were smashed and other JDLers discouraged the police from assisting him.

Once inside the courthouse, the same Crown litany of "not being prepared" was recited. The Prosecution could not even set a date for a preliminary hearing yet! Zundel's attorney, Lauren Marshall, protested that her client "must fight through a mob every time he comes to court."

Thoroughly shaken by the sight of the howling Zionist mob beating cops and Zundelists with equal impunity, Marshall told the court in a trembling voice that she was under threat of death.

Later she would relate to reporters how her seven year old child had earlier answered her home phone to be told, "If your mommy goes to court to defend Zundel she'll be killed."

By holding back adequate police protection, the Canadian Establishment was encouraging the likelihood of this, or Zundel's assassination, knowing fully well that the media would be able to put the blame on the victims.

"It was as if," Zundel afterwards informed his supporters, "the Canadian Establishment were testing our determination, our courage and our sincerity by repeatedly exposing us to the Zionist mob, leaving us to protect ourselves as best we could."

But for the Samisdat freedom fighter, the basic axiom was to find the silver lining in every cloud, to "revalue" every action in favor of one's own objectives:

> If this is the case, we had passed the test with flying colors, for we calmly stood our ground and firmly fought our way into court. Despite our unsympathetic portrayal by media newscasters and commentators, the pictures and sounds of our struggle did not lie: our tiny, valiant band was shown fighting its way steadily up the courthouse steps through the filthy-looking Zionist mob whose screams and howls for blood sounded like some horde of demons from Hades. There was no doubt in the minds of non-Zionist television viewers who the defenders of civilization were on that day, for we received favorable letters and financial support from persons across Canada, most of whom we had not known before and would likely have never known, were it not for the shocking newscasts."

Zundel prepared for his next court rendezvous. Outfitted in snappy high-visibility construction helmets and marching in a casual, but distinctly disciplined formation, Ernst was escorted to court by the largest contingent of his supporters thus far. They had not been cowed by the previous JDL attacks; on the contrary, they had been deeply angered, and they rallied to their leader in the natural way healthy people anywhere would seek to defend a symbol of their people's right to self-determination and defense.

Chartering a full-sized bus, the contingent of forty or so Zundelists were in front of the courthouse and disembarked in a moment. The JDL mob was stunned at the sight of the clean-cut, deliberately paced Samisdat supporters as they escorted Ernst down the street toward the courthouse.

This time however a massive police force was present. Apparently by this juncture the Establishment recognized that not even the lowliest banana republic can afford disrespect for its courts without inviting anarchy. In a polyglot, multi-ethnic, multi-national state like Canada, the Establishment is aware that order must be seen to exist.

The JDL had been given two ample opportunities to cripple or assassinate either Ernst or his attorney. Failing that, they were leashed and held in abeyance.

But mobs have minds of their own, and the "mind" behind the local JDL is that of one Marvin Weinstein (alias "Meir Halevi"). Inside the courthouse Ernst pleaded not-guilty and requested a jury trial. The proceedings had finally begun. At their conclusion, a contingent of seventy police officers escorted the Zundelists onto their chartered bus leaving Weinstein's mob of howling JDLers with no scapegoats to pummel! Incredibly, the Zionists now turned on the media cameramen present who had been photographing their previous brutality, which, in spite of "soothing" and "explanatory" commentary from the TV reporters, still did not give the most complimentary picture of the hirsute Hebrews, whose image as professional persecutees was rapidly dissolving in the public eye. As Ernst described it:

> Denied even one Zundel-supporter to mob, kick and pummel, the Jewish Defense League thugs went wild and began attacking cameramen and reporters from the media. . .Police and public were getting a valuable lesson regarding the true nature of some people who call themselves "Jews."

Samisdat even had its own team of video, audio and still photography recorders, who were at least as thorough as what the media itself furnished at the scene. Throughout his political life, Zundel has insisted that, instead of relying on the System for the record of events and TV "rebuttal" time, dissidents should build their own video network. Instead of relying on media footage of events exclusively, thereby placing dissidents at the mercy of whoever edits it, Zundel provided his own electronic record. It is this sort of autonomy which puts control back in the hands of the activists astute enough to utilize the relatively economical tools of the technological revolution.

The sight of Zundel's disciplined entourage, their attire, conveyance and determination provided visual attractions the media were unable to resist. One newsman remarked that "Zundel's court appearances were all carefully-staged media events" as if Samisdat owned the media!

It should be noted that Ernst did not ask to be prosecuted, did not ask to spend tens of thousands of dollars in legal fees, did not ask to be beaten by a Zionist mob. But once these events were thrust upon him, he refused to passively cooperate as a "good little repentant German." Once the other side had railroaded him into a judicial and mob lynching, he chose to use these factors to his own best advantage in the struggle for truth against a multi-billion dollar oligarchy. Those who insist that Zundel's media "smarts" detract from his dignity as a dissident, are probably not themselves active targets of terrorism, deportation and imprisonment. While Zundel seems to care very little for his own personal safety, he is by no means a dare-devil and has a bigger appetite than most for the joys of this beautiful world.

His reason for being, to his own mind, is to penetrate the iron curtain of lies that permeate our news, entertainment and educational system. To achieve that penetration, he is more than willing to undertake tasks and utilize methods others are uncomfortable with. This is his way. Whether it is right or wrong, it has brought him further into the public eye, with credibility and public interest intact, than any other revisionist activist. He explains his media philosophy in a spring, 1984 broadsheet:

> It is always good for patriots to remember that the media are not closed to us, no matter how much they may disagree with us, provided we understand how to use them to get our message across. . .The JDL. . .by doing their worst, showed us at our best, thereby winning us more public support. This object lesson teaches us that by understanding our opponents, we can actually use their efforts to obtain our objectives. When we know our enemy, the battle is already half won!

In between February and the actual preliminary hearing in June, Samisdat hummed with activity. After defeating the Zionists in the streets, the besieged publishing house was now faced with a courtroom battle where often times deceit, technicalities, tricks and unfair advantage hold sway over facts and truthful exhibits. He was well aware of this risk, but equally aware that the central thesis of the Jewish "Holocaust" claim, the "gassing" allegation, was a ludicrous imposture even some Zionists like Gitta Sereny and Abba Eban were starting to downplay or revise. He wagered that no matter how crooked the trial, some facts would leak out. For this alone, the trial seemed invaluable to the Samisdat movement.

Toward the maximization of that end, Samisdat used its mass mailing expertise to invite the whole world to the Great Holocaust Trial. Massive mailings of invitations to attend, to all major media, were sent from Black Africa, Russia and China to Israel and Europe; from Reuters to Tass.

Next he set about inviting all the revisionist talent on the planet to come forward with primary research, research assistance and testimony at the actual trial. Here was the opportunity for dozens of isolated scholars to come together in a coalition in defense of the historical truth in Canada. Many answered the call and for a time they would transform 206 Carlton St. into a tiny university of forbidden thoughts and suppressed information. Indeed, the actual trial was held on University Ave.

Then he arranged for the cooks, drivers, photographers, translators and security people who would selflessly volunteer their time, coming from the Western hemisphere and all over Europe to lend a hand in a titanic struggle.

Finally he sent out a flyer around the world requesting information for the trial which was divided into 11 categories: Allied brutality, World Leaders who are Known Freemasons, the role of Jews in banking, the Red Cross tracing service in Arolsen, the legal issues of the Nuremberg trials, witnesses to Allied war crimes, actual participants in the war crimes trials, Jewish Population Statistics, Exterminationist claims, contradictory testimony, crimes committed by persons claiming to be "Jews" and assistance in collating the mountain of material.

The word was out, the documents and assistance came pouring in and the June 1984 preliminaries began: for the prosecution, Raul Hilberg, for the defense, Robert Faurisson.

Ditlieb Felderer refers to Dr. Hilberg, a political scientist regarded as the world authority on the Exterminationist theory, as a "theologian," not a historian. For example, when questioned by Attorney Marshall, Hilberg said that the 1944 aerial reconnaissance photographs of Auschwitz which were later analyzed by the CIA in 1978, give massive evidence of crematorium activity, even though they simply do not. An affirmation from a theologian is better than the truth from a heretic, one supposes.

At one point, Hilberg stated that he "could find no satisfactory evidence" of the Germans having made soap from Jewish human fat. But further on he told the court "There may have been, in fact, one or two instances when there was soap production (from human fat). . . but it was not happening as a routine."

Only a theologian or high priest of a cult would first admit that there *is no evidence* for soap from fat having been manufactured, and then on the other hand claim, mystically, that "there may, have been, in fact, one or two instances when there was soap production."

Yes, there "may have been," Raul Hilberg, just as there may have been sky-scrapers on the moon, but without evidence none of these scriptural comment-aries are the province of an historiographer, but rather of a folklorist.

A further indication of the hazy boundary line dividing the thought cops from the men charged with protecting the public's right to know, was revealed by one Sol Littman. Littman is not only a reporter for the national CBC TV network but the Canadian representative of the main "Holocaust" racketeering outfit, the Simon Wiesenthal Center. During the preliminary hearing, while Mr. Littman was presumably impartially reporting the case for millions of Canadians with "fairness," he was caught red-handed by the judge passing notes of advice to the prosecutor! It doesn't get worse than that even in the U.S.S.R. It's probably better, since at least in the Soviet Union most of the people realize the news media is controlled, whereas in Canada there are a good many naive true believers in its "objectivity."

Although attorney Marshall's preliminary examination was competent and she certainly deserved an "A" for her valiant effort, Ernst began the search for an aggressive, civil libertarian barrister to represent him. Failing that, he was considering representing himself.

His trial was slated for December of 1984. His defense team was beginning to take shape around Dr. Faurisson. Witnesses in Germany and the U.S. were lined up. Meanwhile Jim Keegstra, a high school social studies teacher from Alberta, had been fired from his position for having taught an anti-Zionist course, in part touching on the Exterminationist legend. Keegstra's preliminary hearing took place in the summer of 1984. Zundel traveled with his video editor and tech-nician to Alberta to assist in picketing and organizing for Mr. Keegstra. It is here that he saw Douglas Hewson Christie in action in a courtroom setting. The 37 year old attorney from British Columbia is the founder of the Western Canada Concepts party, a group urging a separate nation for the populist west of Canada. A tall, handsome man with a military bearing, Christie impressed Zundel as a tough, principled and learned attroney.

Part of the frenzied Zionist mob who turned their rage on TV cameramen after being prevented from pummeling Zundel as they had two months before, in December, 1983.

COMMISSAR CITRON

''This is a free and democratic country . . .''

It is now the summer of 1984. On July 4, the Institute for Historical Review (IHR) is blown up in a bombing which destroys their $300,000 inventory of banned revisionist books. It is a professional operation executed in under five minutes and defeating the IHR's elaborate burglar and fire alarm system. Irving Rubin, Los Angeles director of the JDL, applauds the bombing but refuses to be specific about his own organization's involvement in the fire, if any.

In September, 1984 Zundel's house is pipebombed, causing damage to a garage door, his car and blasting deadly shrapnel across an alley, knocking holes in a neighbor's brick wall, and damaging cars nearby.

Zundel now approaches Christie about the possibility of representing him in the potentially dangerous Great Holocaust Trial. Christie is new to revisionism and to Zundel but he eagerly agrees if he can obtain credentials to practice in Ontario, which he eventually does.

It is now the waning months of 1984. Christie and Zundel spend ten days at preparation. The pulpits and loudspeakers are shrilly proclaiming that Orwell's prediction had not come to pass: Big Brother had not arrived.

Zundel and his revisionist colleagues knew otherwise. The IHR was burned to the ground, possibly finished. Zundel was under threat of constant assassination and who knows what he would face at the courthouse when the trial actually commenced. There were no active suspects in the bombing of his house, even though a JDL splintergroup claimed "credit."

Meanwhile, Dr. Arthur R. Butz's book, *The Hoax of the 20th Century* had just been seized off library shelves at the Univ. of Calgary by two officers of the Canadian Mounted Police. The circle was tightening. As the final days of December 1984 bowed to a new year, the eyes of the world were turning toward Toronto's York County Court where, for the first time in world history, the Exterminationist legend would go on trial, though Samisdat's foes believe that it is Samisdat that is to be tried. They don't know about Zundel's "judo" yet.

The prosecution is anticipating a quick, two week trial in which the massive weight of the "Holocaust" – all of the "expert" professors, thousands of "eye-witnesses," mountains of "scientific evidence" and the tens of thousands of pages of Nuremberg testimony, will laugh Zundel and his pathetic crew of pseudo-historians and flat-earthists out of public consideration and into the jail cells they so richly deserve.

The media predicted the same scenario and the "smart money" said it was going to be a walkover for the Zionists.

In Washington, my editors at *Spotlight* newspaper assigned me the story. While preparing for the trip to Toronto I stared at a newspaper photograph of the defendant.

Looking at his face I saw something I couldn't exactly assess.

But I knew from studying the countenance of this Swabian peasant that now that he had the momentum he was going to take it for all it was worth. It wouldn't be any walk-over for the Zionists, and by the time Zundel and Christie were finished, the world would be a different place.

These were my thoughts as I boarded my transport on a cold and sunny Sunday morning, January 6, 1985.

II

INQUISITION

There is an attempt—and even the word Satanic cannot describe its evilness—to deny that six million Jews, men, women and children, were led by Nazi Germany and its partners to the pits, the poison-spewing trucks, to the gas chambers. . .
Menachem Begin

If liberty means anything at all, it means the right to tell people what they do not want to hear . . . Is it true about the gas ovens in Poland?
George Orwell

January 7 dawned bitterly cold and sunless in Toronto, but Zundel, Christie, Christie's expert legal assistant Keltie Zubko, and the dozen or so Canadian, German and American patriots who would escort them to court, were in high spirits. All the work and rhetoric, all the confidence in the revisionist case and the belief that a fantastic totem of consensus reality could indeed be slayed by one portly, balding, middle-aged publisher playing the ultimate long-shot, warmed the hearts of those gathered.

The cooks, the maintainence men, the typists, translators and unsung heroes without whom Zundel's warren-like Victorian mansion couldn't have functioned for an hour, gathered near the basement briefing room, to see us off to court. I saw sparkle-eyed elderly German men, and teenaged girls whose hair was so blond it was almost white, filled with an incandescent love. The grizzled, stoop-shouldered mechanics, the not-so-Nordic-looking drivers, the humble jacks of all the trades, labors and struggles that would be required in the seven week marathon that lay ahead, beamed a flood of silent hope and gratitude on to Zundel and Christie.

Arriving at the courthouse, we were greeted by a JDL vigilante mob of some 25 men. In their eyes, shards of pure hatred shot out like flying pieces of glass. They far outnumbered the policemen present. The Establishment had returned to their old tactic. We were to be denied any dignity, any right to walk without violence this day. It was time to run the System-approved terrorist gauntlet yet again. It was outrageous.

I saw these JDL members, their faces screwed into venom-filled masks of fanaticism and ugliness, as the ultimate products of "Holocaust" propaganda. If the internal logic of the accusations of Exterminationism were carried exponentially, this mob was its inevitable outcome. Their violence and terror were "justifiable" by this criterion. The relentless agitation and trauma to which they had been subjected by the media hoax movies and their immediate culture and families, had created these golems, who were so sure of their self-righteous rioting and the necessity for it.

Later, in his summation to the jury, Crown prosecutor Peter Griffiths would claim that revisionism had to be suppressed because if it flourished Jews would be attacked and "loathed." Yet here were the aficionados of Exterminationism about to attack Germans and with very deep loathing, but of course no one is suggesting that we suppress "Holocaust" propaganda as a result of the attacks it encourages—no one save the man on trial this day, and his epigones.

As Zundel's party approached the courthouse, a crush of reporters and cameramen conducted a quick walking interview which was cut short as we grew closer to the mob of crazed Zionist hit-men. It was an odd sensation to know that some of us were going to be beaten today, in full view of a Canadian courthouse, and it would only be "business as usual." The media got out of the way, since these Jews were no respecters of journalists. The skeleton crew of token policemen swallowed hard, knowing they were the patsies for the political decision of the higher-ups, and on we marched toward the courthouse.

"Never again, never again!," the mob screamed with a ferocity and madness I had never before witnessed. With a murderous rage they surged forward in an apparent attempt to tear Ernst limb from limb. On his arm was Christie's female secretary. She wasn't wearing a hardhat. I feared for her life.

Day One: January 7, 1985; Zundel, his female legal researcher on his arm and barrister Douglas Christie (second from the right) about to walk through the JDL gauntlet in front of the York County courthouse. The author (in hood) walks behind Zundel.

Robert Faurisson in his temporary office at Samisdat Publishers during the trial.

Three big Jews made a strenuous effort to knock Zundel's block off with round house punches and uppercuts. Attorney Doug Christie ducked quickly as a punch from a heavy-set JDLer just missed his jaw. The Zundel men on the outside flank separating the legal team and defendant from the rioters, were viciously punched and slapped by the Jews. One 60 year old German man was slammed to the ground. I could see blood on his forehead. More punches rained in on Zundel but his friends in the front managed to absorb them instead.

Seeing that the police were doing next to nothing, Zundel's "boys" as he called them, decided that they had to fight back or there might be serious injury to Ernst or the one brave lawyer in all of Canada who would represent him with vigor.

One East-German slammed his fist into the face of Meir Halevi, the JDL leader, who fell to the ground, losing his glasses. A Zundelist from Ottawa and a moving man from Toronto knocked two other Zionists into stone pillars and a glass retaining wall and down the Zionists went. By doing so, they cleared the way for the Zundel party to finally get in to the relative safety of the courthouse. Four Jews, including Halevi, were arrested on wrist-slapping charges. They had unquestionably assaulted—even tried to kill a Canadian lawyer and his client and legal secretary—yet not even a charge of assault was lodged. Instead they were arrested for "disturbing the peace." They were later cleared of all charges, of course. Subsequent newspaper accounts made ridiculously Orwellian references to the four "defense league" members arrested. They had attacked, they had rioted, they had terrorized but they are called "defense league members." As journalist Doug Collins would later inform the court, their real name should be the Jewish Attack League.

Inside the court Christie was able to make an issue out of the ugly JDL riot, noting that its obvious intent was to intimidate Zundel's legal defense into quitting. He told reporters during a recess, "I've never seen people beaten on the steps of a courthouse like that with absolute impunity before." The national evening TV news carried embarrassing photos of JDL members sprawled on the ground after having been tamed by the Zundelists. But while issuing a restraining order against further JDL riots (how big of him), presiding Judge Hugh Locke accused Zundel and his men of provoking the JDL by wearing protective hard hats!

Locke next ruled that "free speech was not absolute" and that the recently enacted Canadian Charter of Rights (similar to the U.S. Bill of Rights), did not forbid the trial. This rendered the high-sounding "guarantees" of the much touted charter for civil liberties, into just a meaningless scrap of paper.

Locke also refused to permit Christie to question potential jurors about their views on "Holocaust" allegations, their biases—if any—toward Germans and their affiliations with Zionists, Jews and Freemasons. Just prior to the Zundel trial, Jewish abortionist Dr. Henry Morgenthaler was tried for violations of the abortion laws and his attorneys were permitted to ask four probing questions of potential jurors and to exclude Roman Catholics and others deemed holding preconceptions about Morgenthaler.

Whereas the Crown had an unlimited number of jury challenges, Christie was left with four and these were to be used without in any way substantively questioning potential jurors. Christie was restricted to asking them to repeat

Jewish group attacks Zundel and followers on way to trial

By KIRK MAKIN

Members of the Jewish Defence League screaming anti-Nazi slogans attacked a group which questions whether the Nazis killed six million Jews in Europe, outside Toronto's downtown County Courthouse this morning.

Ernst Zundel, a 46-year-old Toronto man charged with spreading false news, and about 15 followers clad in yellow hardhats were set upon as they walked hastily in a box-like formation toward the courthouse.

About 15 Metro Toronto police could not hold back many of the 25 members of the defence league and several punches landed on Mr. Zundel's followers.

During the 30-second melee police tackled a couple of the attackers to the ground.

Rhythmic chants of "Never again, never again," changed quickly into obscenities and taunts.

There were no apparent serious injuries. A police spokesman said four defence league members were charged with causing a disturbance.

Inside, a packed courtroom watched as Mr. Zundel was arraigned on two charges of spreading false news which he knew would cause or was likely to cause mischief to racial or social tolerance.

The charges relate to two articles, West, War and Islam, and Did 6 Million Really Die?

Defence counsel Douglas Christie then made several pre-trial motions before County Court Judge Hugh Locke regarding the constitutionality of the charges and the process by

Ernst Zundel

which the jury will be selected.

Mr. Christie, who recently defended Albertan Jim Keegstra in a similar case, flew from Victoria, B.C., to represent Mr. Zundel.

In an interview, Mr. Christie decried the violence outside the courtroom.

"I've never seen people beaten on the steps of a courthouse like that with absolute impunity," he said.

The *Globe and Mail*, January 7, 1985.

The Jewish stormtroops were cleared of all charges in a subsequent trial.

information they had already given regarding their names and occupations. In a trial that would put a premium on mind-reading abilities, Christie was supposed to "discern" who the objective jurors were. Hence the 10 man, two woman jury that was picked, largely by the prosecution, may have contained Jews or Freemasons or their relatives and business associates, as well as confirmed anti-German bigots. No matter, the show must go on.

Before the jury was impaneled, Christie played videotapes for the judge on a courtroom TV, giving examples of gross misrepresentation and outright deceitful characterizations of Samisdat by the press. The judge did not however sequester the jury in hotel rooms under orders not to watch TV during the trial, as was done in the far less emotional and controversial Von Bulow trial in the U.S., in May. Locke claimed such a move would insult the jury's intelligence. During the trial, anti-German hate movies such as *The Execution, The Belarus File* and other Hollywood "Holocaust" hate-Germans hype, were broadcast on TV. These movies constituted blatant propaganda for the prosecution. They were heavily advertised and noted in the press, and broadcast across North America. It seems likely that some jurors watched them, much to the detriment of their ability to be fair.

The prosecution was also permitted to show a discredited 1945 Allied propaganda film in the courtroom. On the other hand, not one visual exhibit, from the very important aerial reconnaissance photos taken of Auschwitz in 1944, to an expertly crafted scale model of this camp; to Ditleb Felderer's expertly detailed photographs documenting Auschwitz fakes and prisoner amenities, were permitted as exhibits for the defense by Judge Locke. This crippling restriction seriously hampered the testimony of Dr. Faurisson for example, which bears greatly on the reconnaissance photos. As usual, the opposition knew that control of the visual imagery, whether in popular culture or a criminal law courtroom, is vital to the continuation of the myth.

Before the judge, but with the jury absent, audio and videotapes of JDL violence were played. In one grisly, 20 minute audio tape compiled from Ernst's recording of Jewish hate calls he has received over the years, the most filthy and blood-curdling epithets were heard. Zundel would be "cut into little pieces" or castrated. His family would be raped, the callers said. This did nothing to sway either the hostile judge or the wind-up media into understanding that the tide had shifted and Germans were now the subjects of tremendous hate. The fact didn't fit the media stereotype so it had to be ruled out of cognition.

The first witness for the prosecution was Sgt. Ron Williams, a researcher for the police department's Attorney General's support staff, who had supposedly been rigorously analyzing *Did Six Million Really Die?* to reveal its contradictions and mistakes. But upon cross-examination, Christie made a monkey out of Williams, drawing from him the admission that he hadn't even read the whole booklet during a "seven month investigation", and had not bothered to check its references against the original sources cited. Williams also admitted that he was a practicing Freemason. How was it that a Freemason could give "unbiased" testimony against a man who was also being charged with writing a pamphlet, *The West, War and Islam*, highly critical of Freemasons?

Next on the stand was a 56 year-old Hungarian Jew, Arnold Friedman. He was touted as an "eyewitness" to homicidal gassings at Auschwitz, where he had been interned as a teenager. According to the news media, people like Friedman are the sort of hard facts-oriented truth-tellers who can "blow away" with their righteous testimony those "damned liars" who deny gas chambers.

According to Prosecutor Peter Griffiths, Friedman was the type of person whose feelings would be hurt if "Holocaust" doubters continued to be allowed to question the unquestionable.

Fortunately for history and the cause of Truth, which is more important than *anyone's* "feelings," not to mention the totally neglected feelings of the German nation wrongfully accused, Douglas Christie, the "Black Sheep of the Canadian Bar" *was able* to ask some questions of Mr. Friedman. As revisionists have always pointed out, the deluded finger-pointers can only get away with their insane gassing accusations as long as they are protected from critical scrutiny by a cellophane of media insulation.

We are ordered to accept with blind faith whatever "eyewitnesses" such as Mr. Friedman say, on pain of being accused of being "anti-Semitic" or, in the words of Menachem Begin, "Satanic." According to the Establishment, only someone who was insane or anti-Semitic would dare to contradict or doubt Jewish "eyewitnesses." Let us see who really is insane.

Mr. Friedman testified that while in Auschwitz he saw "fourteen foot flames" shooting out of the crematorium chimneys. He also gave sworn testimony that he was able to tell whether the Nazis were burning fat Jewish Hungarians or skinny Jewish Poles by looking at the different colors of the smoke and flames coming out of the crematorium.

This is the sworn testimony Friedman gave in a trial where a man faced two years imprisonment based on these statements. And who knows, with the increasingly wild exaggerations and tall tales that are routinely spun about the "Holocaust" in the media, maybe some people would believe that Mr. Friedman's hallucination about color-coded flames was real. Doug Christie was not one of them however:

> I put it to you that you don't really understand anything about crematoria. . . because that is quite wrong, sir. . . I suggest it is quite impossible for smoke to come from a crematoria from human beings.

Christie then cited the scientific fact that crematoria were specifically designed *not* to give off either smoke, flame, ashes or odors. It is *technically impossible* for crematoria to emit them.

Friedman tried to save face by claiming that the German crematoria at Auschwitz were not "ordinary" crematoria. It is at this point that certain major American news media outlets such as the *Boston Globe* and *Chicago Tribune* ended their report of the Friedman-Christie exchange. By doing so, they gave the impression that Friedman was right about what he claimed to have seen— 14 foot flames and smoke bellowing out of "special" crematorium chimneys right after trainloads of people were unloaded. This a textbook example of how the media omits vital information, and reports only part of the news to protect the Zionist side of every story. Stopping the account here gives the impression— and wouldn't you just know it?—that those sinister Nazis even went so far as to build "special" crematorium that could do what no other crematorium were designed to do—give off smoke, flames and odors to scare the hapless Jews "before they were gassed" and attract attention from Allied bombers.

In reality however, the rest of this exchange that wasn't reported in the U.S. Establishment media was the best part.

Mr. Christie produced the *patent* for the crematorium built at Auschwitz by the firm of Topf and Son. The patent clearly showed that these were very ordinary crematorium scientifically incapable of emitting any flames or smoke, (crematorium existed at Auschwitz in the first place as a sanitary means of handling the dead, including German dead, who had expired from typhus and other disease outbreaks. At its height, the inmate population at Auschwitz reached 200,000).

Now Mr. Friedman was in serious difficulty. Jews in the courtroom fidgeted and twitched nervously as he disconsolately agreed that perhaps Jews were not being burned in crematoria buildings. Then Mr. Friedman made an even more startling confession to a question from Christie.

Asked the young lawyer, "Couldn't there have been many other explanations (for the smoke and flames)?"

"Yes, there could have," Friedman admitted. "If I had listened to you at the time when I was listening to other people (in the camp), I might have listened to you. But at the time I listened to them."

In other words, Mr. Friedman, a frightened boy at Auschwitz, had had his head filled with the wildest of rumors. These were then probably compounded by watching post-war Hollywood fantasy movies such as *The Wall* which graphically depict massive crematoria chimneys belching clouds of smoke. The constant images of Hollywood fantasies about Auschwitz mixed with rumors and adolescent credulity yield "eyewitness testimony."

This writer takes no comfort in Mr. Friedman's discredited "eyewitness testimony." Friedman is in some ways himself a victim of the "Holocaust" hoax. But the fact is, *he* set himself up as a man so sure of himself that with his words he would put a dissident publisher behind bars.

Readers will note that the media continues to repeat the nonsense about smoke and ash coming from concentration camp crematorium. As recently as the April 23, 1985 edition of the *NY Times* we read how one Pearl Herskovic says she saw her whole family go up in "billowing smoke" from an Auschwitz crematorium chimney. She says she stood there watching the smoke when suddenly her family's "ashes began to fall on my arm." Here is the miracle folklore and fantasy masquerading as unchallenged, irrefutable fact which is able to seem credible only because it is shielded from all contradiction by Zionist media control. Scientific fact and technical impossibility are no obstacle to the beliefs of an irrational cult whose "truth" is drummed into people's heads through the brainwashing power of endless repetition and the suppression of contrary information.

We can see this in action in the *NY Times* p. 2 article on Zundel entitled, "Anti-Semite on Trial, but Did Ontario Blunder?" (Feb. 15, 1985). If we ever needed proof about the deceitfulness of this Jewish-owned newspaper it will probably not surface any clearer than in the following example.

In his article for the *Times*, reporter Douglas Martin did not report even the first half of the Friedman-Christie exchange as had some other U.S. papers. Instead, Martin gave it the following fascinatingly revealing half-a-sentence: "The upshot (of the trial) has been a bizarre flurry of newspaper headlines calling the existence of crematoriums in Nazi death camps a theory not a fact. . . ."

Clever, eh? The *NY Times* is telling its millions of trusting readers that Christie and Friedman were clashing over whether or not *there were crematoriums in the camp: whether or not they "existed" at all*. But as we have seen, this was *not the issue whatsoever*. The issue pertained to what the crematoria gave off, not whether there were crematoria in Auschwitz.

The specific newspaper headline mentioning a crematoria *theory* referred to by Times reporter Martin, is from the Jan. 12 Toronto *Globe and Mail*. If Mr. Martin bothered to read that article he would have known that the "theory" at issue was the theory that crematoria give off smoke and flame. One trembles at the possibility that Martin did actually read the *Globe and Mail* article in its entirety and wrote his article anyway, knowing it contained a lie.

The *NY Times*, in its desperation to portray revisionists as stereotypical, dehumanized crackpots, had doctored its trial report with a little "false news" of its own. Accurate reporting would have damaged the myth too much.

Only four days into the Great Holocaust Trial, and the supposedly overwhelming "mountain of evidence" backing up the Extermination hoax was unraveling like an old pair of pants.

Friedman's folly was followed by Sgt. Roy Bassett of the Toronto Police, testifying on behalf of Freemasonry with regard to the charges leveled by the defendant in his "West, War and Islam" broadsheet, to the effect that the masons were a secret society bent on world domination.

Sgt. Bassett vehemently denied that Freemasonry was a secret society. But when ordered by Mr. Christie to reveal the secret oaths used by the masons in Bassett's own lodge, the police seargent refused. The defense attorney reminded him that he was under oath and compelled to reveal the whole truth. Bassett adamantly refused to disclose the secret oath.

Christie asked the judge to please inform Bassett of his duty as a witness under oath. Judge Locke refused Christie's request saying that the question was irrelevant. The secret that wasn't a secret remained secret. Masonic oaths took precedence over court oaths in Judge Locke's courtroom.

After Bassett came Ignatz Fulop, another Auschwitz "eyewitness" who spun the usual inflated fantasies about seeing ten people hung on a rope every morning before breakfast. His memory failed him with regard to the loading platform at Auschwitz. He claims there was no platform, but in fact, by May of 1944, the time Fulop was there, there was indeed a platform.

Fulop, another one of the millions who somehow miraculously survived the "ruthlessly efficient Nazi extermination machine" gave inadvertantly important supporting testimony for what the Germans and revisionists say really did go on in the camps: that people really were bathed and showered, clothes and bedding had to be fumigated with insecticide, all as a means of preventing the deadly typhus plague which was killing Germans and Jews alike, (there was no cure for typhus—carried by body lice—back then. One either recovered through fighting if off with one's own natural immunological defenses or one died, as many Jews *and* camp guards did. Even Dr. Mengele, the camp doctor, contracted typhus but survived it).

Zundel's enemies eagerly anticipated the testimony of the next witness. If Christie had managed to "take advantage" of the "understandable" befuddlement of former concentration camp inmates, he and his German client would soon get their comeuppance, reasoned the Israel lobby, with the testimony of the next individual.

He was none other than Dr. Raul Hilberg, professor of Political Science at the University of Vermont. Reporter Bradley Smith writes of him, "No one on the planet is considered a greater authority on the 'Holocaust' than Dr. Raul Hilberg, author of *The Destruction of the European Jews*. That's why the Canadian government chose him to testify for the State at the Great Canadian Show Trial . . . ."

In less than two weeks, the Zundel trial was now confronting the apex of the "Holocaust." If gas chamber doubters are in general confronted by a "mountain of evidence proving the 'Holocaust' which no one can deny," here now was the world's greatest expert on that pile of evidence. How could Christie, Zundel or any revisionist stand a chance before Hilberg, a professional witness accustomed to giving testimony all over the world, unflappable and calm under fire and the "world's greatest authority" on the whole subject?

Hilberg began by describing himself to the court as an interpreter of documents and not an on-site forensic investigator of the concentration camps. In fact it was *18 years* after the publication of his "definitive" "Holocaust" history, before he actually got around to *visiting* the camps he had written so extensively about, taking a *one day tour* in 1979 of Auschwitz and Treblinka.

Hilberg testified that his principle concentration was on documents. The principle document upon which Hilberg's Extermination theory is based, is the "confession" of SS Obersturmbanfuehrer Kurt Gerstein. It consists of seven and one-half pages of text. Hilberg cites from this document at length (ten times), in his history of the "Holocaust." (Gerstein died under mysterious circumstances while awaiting a war crimes trial). Gerstein was the key source for Hilberg's entire thesis.

In his seven and one-half page confession, Gerstein supposedly swore that:

- "700 to 800" Jews were squeezed into a gas chamber at Belzec measuring 25 square meters. This is the size of about a two car garage.

- That Adolf Hitler was personally at a homicidal "gassing" camp.

- 25 million people were gassed.

Dr. Arthur R. Butz, the much-maligned author of *The Hoax of the 20th Century*, has described Gerstein's confession as "absolutely insane" and pointed out that it was unforgivable that Hilberg would use such an obviously spurious "confession" as a source. Butz was pilloried as an "anti-Semite" for saying this.

Now, thanks to the Zundel trial, Doug Christie could finally confront Hilberg on Gerstein. Fired Christie, "Don't you think it reflects on an author that some statements are absolutely ridiculous?".

Hilberg admitted that Gerstein was extremely unreliable in certain passages of the confession. But he defended his use of Gerstein's testimony: "I realized, of course, what kind of person he was and I did not rely on any statements I regarded as imaginative or incredible. I think he was given to great excitability. What can you say?, Hilberg asked.

"You could say he was crazy," the defense attorney shot back.

Hilberg attempted to explain, "I'm not a psychiatrist. . I'm not making diagnoses here. I would not characterize him as totally rational".

When Hilberg stated that he "did not rely on any statements" by Gerstein that he "regarded as imaginative or incredible" he means that he *edited out of his history book those statements of Gerstein's that would have seemed too insane to his readers and which would have cast doubt on the parts of the confession Hilberg did use.*

Even worse than this logic-chopping, Hilberg never informed his readers that he had edited out statements Gerstein had made that were insane. Instead, he gave the appearance, through clever editing, that Gerstein was a sensible and reliable person. And by means of the Gerstein confession, Prof. Hilberg accuses the German people of mass murder. Bradley Smith:

> As Kurt Gerstein was certifiably nuts, and as he was demonstrably a liar, and as Professor Raul Hilberg quoted Gerstein "10 times" in his *The Destruction of European Jews* as being a credible eyewitness to those "gassings" . . . how many kinds of intellectual fraud has Hilberg involved himself with, and how did he ever manage to make his way to Toronto to toady to the State censors when everywhere he goes he must have to wade bum-deep through this kind of cow flop?

The nationally circulated *Globe and Mail* newspaper headlined the story of Hilberg's shamefaced admissions as "Holocaust scholar quoted 'madman,' publishing trial told". Suddenly Hilberg was complaining to the court that the trial was taking too long and he had to get back to his college classes in Vermont!

Next, Zundel's defense lawyer requested that Hilberg offer some scientific proof of the Germans having killed millions of Jews with poison gas. If there is a "mountain of proof" of the exterminations having taken place as the news media incessantly reminds us in a thousand books, movies, newspaper articles, TV specials and radio shows, surely there is some technical data and reports available giving this forensic proof. We shouldn't have to rely on "confessions" alone to uphold the "facts" of mass murder by gassing, there should be scientific proof.

Christie: "Can you give me one scientific report that shows the existence of gas chambers anywhere in Nazi-occupied territory?".

Hilberg: "I'm at a loss".

Christie: "You are (at a loss) because you can't. I want one report, before, during or after the war that shows that someone was killed by the use of those gases," Christie challenged.

Hilberg: "You want an autopsy (report) and I know of no autopsy."

"Holocaust" historian Dr. Raul Hilberg

He could not provide even one scientific report showing the existence of homicidal gas chambers. Hilberg: "I'm at a loss."

Big Brother Marvin Weinstein, alias "Meir Halevi"

"We are not harrassing this person (Zundel), we are simply keeping him under surveillance."

Hilberg told the court he could not think of any reason why a scientist would undertake such a study.

Later, the Battling Barrister confronted Hilberg with information from U.S. Judge Edward L. Van Roden published in 1949, showing that German prisoners had been tortured by American soldiers. Judge Van Roden stated that 137 German soldiers that he investigated "had been kicked in the testicles beyond repair." The judge also concluded that the Americans had shoved burning matches under German POW's fingernails and broke their jaws during the so-called "Dachau" war crimes trials. Judge Van Roden had been a member of the Simpson —Van Rhoden Commission, a panel which had looked into the torture of German POW's. His findings were published nationally in 1949 in *The Progressive* magazine. Hilberg told the court he was unaware of the judge's report.

"You set yourself up as an expert," Christie admonished, "to say that articles my client published are fanciful. Then when I asked you about books, you say you haven't read them," Christie accused.

"You don't have to answer that!" presiding Judge Locke snapped on Prof. Hilberg's behalf.

Here was the world's "greatest expert" on the "Holocaust" admitting there wasn't a single shred of scientific or technical evidence – not even an autopsy – to back up the incredible claims.

Now the Exterminationists were getting panicky. Their entire cult was being revealed for the cheap media hoax that it was: A fraud built on "testimonies" and "confessions" and movies, books and articles based on the confessions and the testimonies.

But when asked for some hard evidence – anything, no matter how small in a legend and myth so utterly vast – the "Holocaust" expert who was supposed to make a fool of Zundel made a fool of himself.

How many of those who accuse revisionists of being totally wrong for questioning the gas chamber claims, even know this fact? There sat Hilberg in the witness box admitting what naive millions of people would never have imagined: that there is no real proof apart from lies scribbled on paper. "No scientific proof of the Holocaust" the Canadian newspaper headlines bannered, as Hilberg skulked back to his professor's post in Vermont.

At Zundel headquarters spirits were understandably high. But Zundel himself seemed to be guarded in his enthusiasms, as if he had a premonition of something the rest of us did not. Small donations from working class people in North America and Europe were arriving, the circle of supporters in the house and in Toronto as a whole had a bounce to their steps and Samisdat was humming with activity as the legal team headed by Doug and assisted by Keltie poured over piles of documents in the cavernous living room.

Guiding the revisionist research team was Dr. Robert Faurisson, professor of Documents and Textual Critique at the University of Lyon in France, co-author of *Verite historique ou verite politique?* and who, together with Dr. Arthur R. Butz of Northwestern University and Dr. James J. Martin, is in the *avant-garde* of academic revisionism. Assisting him was his good friend and colleague, Ditlieb Felderer, author of *Anne Frank's Diary a Hoax* and the leading forensic investigator of Auschwitz, having performed painstaking research at that facility in the course of 27 visits. Other members of the research team on the scene included

Udo Walendy, John Ball, Tudal Rudolf, Juergen Neuman, Dr. Charles Weber, Robert Miller, David McCalden, Hans von der Heide and Eric Thomson. Assisting from Evanston, Illinois was Dr. Butz and from New Jersey, Friedrich P. Berg. Their background preparations reached a fever pitch as the prosecution brought in their next "big gun," the angry old man of Exterminationism, the confirmed leftist and German-baiter, Rudolf Vrba (pronounced Vur-ba).

Vrba claimed to have been in Auschwitz and Majdanek concentration camps until April of 1944. Vrba's account of killing gas chambers for humans made its way to the War Refugee Board, where it became one of the most crucial cornerstones of the entire gassing and "abandonment of the Jews" thesis. Vrba's report is part of an exhibit at Auschwitz. He testified against Germans during the Auschwitz trials in West Germany. His book, *I Cannot Forgive*, is holy scripture, revered for its "honesty" and depth of righteous anger at the "Nazi beasts," throughout the world.

In a letter to Christie outlining Vrba's qualifications as a prosecution witness, Crown Prosecutor Griffiths wrote on Jan. 9, "I understand he (Vrba), can give direct evidence of the existence of (homicidal) gas chambers and the numbers killed at Auschwitz."

In other words, Rudolf Vrba was another "Holocaust heavyweight," idolized in the media as a virtually infallible spokesman, martyr and conscience-of-the-world.

Now he would face the Zundel juggernaut and Doug Christie's Knight's lance. The revisionists were on a roll. Because Vrba was a known German-hater, Christie, Faurisson and the research team, including Ernst, were eager to confront him.

At first it was tough going. Vrba was an insulting and disrespectful witness. It was obvious he had nothing but contempt for Zundel's lawyer and for the defendant himself.

Dr. Faurisson, sitting at the defense table, was patient. Ernst and Keltie took copious notes. Faurisson was preparing the net, biding his time. Meanwhile Christie was almost as caustic as the witness, at one point suggesting that Vrba must have used trick memory techniques to keep his lies straight.

"Should I bring you six million bodies here that are the proof?", Vrba wisecracked.

"I'd be content with just one autopsy report," retorted the attorney.

Vrba testified that 150,000 French Jews were gassed at Auschwitz. But Christie produced documentation to show that the entire number of Jews deported from France was only 75,721. Vrba was asked to explain how he arrived at the figure of 150,000 French Jews being at Auschwitz alone. Vrba's "scientific" method for figuring this number consisted of his having listened to the language the inmates spoke, and by examining what style of luggage they carried.

As Christie's lance drew more blood from Vrba, Vrba took refuge in the last resort of the saintly "survivors" when confronted with the truth about themselves and their Cult of the Big Lie.

"I am saying to you that to consider a person who fought the Nazis is a liar, is a misuse of the free courts of Canada" bellowed Vrba. He is suggesting here that Christie be forbidden from asking the kind of tough, skeptical questions

EXPERT'S ADMISSION:
Some gas death 'facts' nonsense

By MARIA BOHUSLAWSKY
Staff Writer

A Holocaust expert yesterday admitted at the Ernst Zundel trial that some of his facts on gas chambers came from a man who spoke "pure nonsense."

"I think that Gerstein was somewhat given to great excitability," Dr. Raúl Hilberg, a professor at the University of Vermont, told the 12-member jury.

"He was capable of adding imagination to fact."

Kurt Gerstein was an SS officer in charge of delivering gases to Nazi concentration camps.

He swore affadavits at the Nuremberg trials which tried and convicted some accused war criminals.

Under cross-examination by Zundel's lawyer, Doug Christie, of Victoria, B.C., Hilberg admitted he quoted Gerstein 10 times in his book *The Destruction of the European Jews* to describe the use of gas chambers to kill Jews in camps which existed for their extermination.

ERNST ZUNDEL
Holocaust booklets

However, he said he edited out the parts of Gerstein's statement that were "pure nonsense," using only that which was "credible and corroborated.

"He's an important witness for the fact of the existance of these camps, especially Belzec, and the gassings that took place there," said Hilberg.

Gerstein swore that 700 to 800 people were packed onto spaces which were 25 square metres.

"Well, I have made calculations and it's quite amazing how many people you can squeeze into a space," said Hilberg.

He dismissed as "totally false" a statement by Gerstein that Adolf Hitler attended gassings.

Hilberg also admitted that no specific record exists of what Hitler's orders regarding the Jews were and whether in fact he had officially ordered them murdered.

He said a general's report on Hitler's order exists.

"There is no precise, clear answer as to what the specific wording was," he said. "This order was to the armed forces and the einsatzgruppen (mobile death units.)"

Zundel, 46, a Toronto publisher, has pleaded not guilty to two counts of publishing statements he knew were false and would incite people to commit mischief.

In one he disputes the number of Jews who died during World War II and that the Nazi's had a deliberate extermination policy.

In the other he says Zionists, bankers, Communists and Freemasons are involved in a world-wide conspiracy to promote Jews to power to further Zionist goals.

The trial continues.

The Toronto Sun, **January 17, 1985.**

that reveal lies and liars. Imperial personalities like Vrba are not to be questioned, only worshipped and followed blindly. Hosanna.

If Christie could have been muzzled, some of Vrba's credibility might have been salvaged. But it was not to be. Vrba's downfall came when Dr. Faurisson noted Vrba's testimony that he had seen an SS man pour poison gas through a roof hole in an upper-level gas chamber and then jauntily climb down.

Christie forced Vrba to admit that the "chamber" in question was not a homicidal gas chamber at all but a mortuary and that it was not up high enough that someone had to climb down from it, because it was in fact located partially underground. Vrba said his error was "in good faith."

Then, suddenly there came a stunning series of confessions from Vrba about his book, *I Cannot Forgive*, the "eyewitness" proof of homicidal gassings that we hear so much about. The "I saw it with my own eyes—so how can *you* deny it?" dogma that flourishes so well in a media vacuum where no reporters dare scrutinize a certified saintly "Holocaust Survivor," was about to take a beating.

Vrba actually confessed that his book was "an artistic picture. . . not a document for a court." He agreed that he had *never actually witnessed anybody being gassed to death*, but had heard rumors! He further admitted that his written and pictorial descriptions of Auschwitz crematoria were a result of guessing, based on "what I heard it might look like" (Cf. *Toronto Sun*, Jan. 24, 1985, p. 52).

Trying to keep up some semblance of a front, Vrba squeaked that his mistakes were due to his "great urgency" to warn his fellow Jews.

Vrba had turned out to be as big a fraud as Hilberg. No wonder the Zionists use every conceivable legal, economic, political, defamatory and violent ploy they can to stop the questioning of "The Holocaust." Here were the top experts tumbling like bowling pins before the questions of an impecunious young attorney and an obscure French professor.

The crack in the cosmic egg kept on cracking at the Great Holocaust Trial.

Back at Samisdat Headquarters, the Zundelists were ecstatic. There were group sing-alongs around the piano, toasts of good cheer and excited anticipation of what would happen next, of what other sacred cow would tumble into the dust.

Each evening after the full day's session in court was completed, Ernst and Doug held a debriefing in the basement-barracks. Ernst went over the main points, Doug fleshed out other highlights and the troops laughed and cheered. There was no doubt to anyone in the room that, win, lose, or draw, we had already won! The jury might be crooked or some last minute tearful stunt might be pulled, but the revelations so far were historic. The P.T. Barnums of Consensus Reality might suppress them in the U.S., but ultimately they would stand as crucial revelations to those whose thinking was not the prisoner of Newspeak linguistic-cognitive limitation and stereotyped "hunt for my pet concepts" mentation.

The trial was taking place in the best Canadian city for such an event, Toronto, home of several television networks and the nationally circulated *Globe and Mail*. Toronto is Canada's media center. It was being held at an excellent time of the year, the winter months of January and February when Canadians by the millions watched the greatest amount of TV newscasts.

On TV newscasts at 5:30, 6, 6:30, 7, 10, and 11 p.m., the Zundel victories were broadcast coast-to-coast to a nation hungry for suppressed truth. The reporting was somewhat hostile and twisted, but fundamentally accurate enough to convey the essential impression that this was no walkover, that something was "wrong" from the point of view of the Establishment, that Zundel was not only holding his ground but was inflicting serious damage on the myth.

In the courthouse hallway one day, one of Zundel's supporters, an ordinary working man, was approached by an anonymous individual who handed him a fat envelope and curtly told him to "give it to Zundel." It was delivered in the court room during a recess. It contained $1,000 in cash.

Everywhere in the West, the cobwebbed inaction resulting from decades of frustrations, feelings of defeat, hopelessness and angst were dissolving. People everywhere were inspired by Zundel's example and by the example of idealistic Douglas Christie, risking his career to take on the gigantic power of the Zionist lobby.

At this juncture, the reader may be wondering, "If all of these highly embarrasing revelations of what a bunch of phonies all these 'eyewitnesses' and "experts" were came out, how is it that the jury convicted Zundel?"

It is necessary to point to the emotionally exploitative manipulations that took place in the trial, the climate of fear that even the judge admitted when he said "everybody's been threatened", including the jury.

The "Holocaust" is the closest thing to a state religion that the West has seen since medieval times. The majority of people are almost hopelessly brainwashed, frightened to death of the "poor, persecuted and powerless Zionists" and simply incapable of going against the massive power of the State, the Press and the Jewish lobby.

Keep in mind however that Zundel's own writing about the Jews in his essay *The West, War and Islam*, was vindicated, with a "not-guilty" verdict. I believe this was a token of esteem for Zundel and the result of a jury compromise between at least one or two jurors who were decidedly sympathetic. This sympathy will be pointed out in the testimony of Ditlieb Felderer.

My main point however pertains to the supremely corrupt and decadent state of our people in the 1980's. Ten angels from heaven appearing to swear that homicidal gas chambers are a cheap con would not sway many of our indoctrinated brethren. The quality of the people we attract to our cause is, at this point in time, far more important than the quantity of people. Quality people will study the record of the Great Zundel Trial and use these revelations to ultimately expose this evil swindle of Exterminationism, while the masses will still be nestling their six packs in front of the boob tube, believing every word of the latest "Holocaust" flick.

Another interesting witness for the prosecution was Dennis Urstein, an "eyewitness" with the "positive proof." He claimed he saw bodies gassed with Zyklon B hauled out of the "gas chamber." He described the bodies as being "greyish-greenish" in color. Persons who have died from Zyklon B poisoning turn a bright cherry red.

In assisting with the disposal of bodies in the gas chamber it seems that Urstein wore no protective clothing. If this was the case he would have died too. Urstein also claimed with absolute certainty that 154 of his family died in the

"Holocaust" but he had the greatest of difficulty naming even 20 of them. Of the 20 that he said died at the hands of the Nazis, one of these actually died in the U.S. in the late 1970's.

Henry Leader was another "eyewitness" who couldn't get the body color of the supposed Zyklon B gas victims correct. He didn't even agree with Urstein's gray-green color. Leader came up with a new one: Blue. Leader grabbed for all the soap opera gusto that he could, appealing to the jury and courtroom about the ordeal of his testimony and how terrible it was that these rotten revisionists forced him to repeat all his dreadful memories, as he chomped on his "heart pills." In reality though, Mr. Leader had eagerly *volunteered* to testify.

The next witness pertained to the Crown's desire to convict Zundel for having written his *West, War and Islam* broadside. In his work, the author asserted that an unholy alliance of masons, Marxists, Zionists and bankers were seeking to dominate the world.

John Burnett, senior vice-president and general counsel for the Royal Bank of Canada told the court rather lamely, "If we're involved in sponsoring and supporting communist governments, so is the Canadian government."

Doug Christie pointed out to the jury how large loans made to Third World nations by multi-national banking houses threatened the stability of the world. Burnett defended his bank's refusal to do business with South Africa on a normal basis because South Africa was "immoral." Burnett's bank does quite a bit of business with communist slave governments, which is not immoral according to Mr. Burnett.

The Crown prosecutor's case was slowly dissolving around him. Zionists condemned him at every turn as incompetent, he lost considerable weight, and at one point Judge Hugh Locke himself had to take over part of the prosecution, asking questions of defense witnesses that Griffiths had forgotten to pose. It was humiliating for Griffiths, highly irregular of the judge and extremely worrisome to the holy ones who were now beginning to turn on fellow holy one Sabina Citron, and her "Holocaust Remembrance Association", for having forced the trial in the first place.

The Exterminationist ace-in-the-hole has always been Hollywood, so as the final "argument" which closed their case, Griffiths showed the jury the movie *Nazi Concentration Camps*, which was filmed in 1945 by Hollywood director George Stevens. It is filled with inaccuracies (such as that gas chambers existed in camps where even the *Zionists now admit* they did not) and maximum exploitation of scenes of piles of bodies to "prove" the means of death (do piles of bodies prove the bodies were "gassed?").

But the defense was not allowed to show the jury a single visual exhibit. Finally, after weeks of hearing from prosecution witnesses who revealed the most we know about the hoax since the publication of Dr. Butz's *Hoax of the 20th Century*, it was the revisionists turn at bat.

The leader of Zundel's research team, Dr. Robert Faurisson of the University of Lyon, was recognized as an expert witness on document authentication by the court, but he was forbidden from referring to the slides and photographs which are the cornerstone of his argument concerning what really occurred at Auschwitz. Dr. Faurisson has been studying the homicidal gassing hoax for

Researcher Keltie Zubko (L) and attorney Douglas Christie.

Samisdat's legal braintrust.

The defendant (third from the right) with assistant toting documentary files.

In the wake of bombings, beatings and death threats, Zundel and his legal team always walked to and from the courthouse amid a huddle of helmeted supporters. Judge Locke termed the helmets a provocation.

25 years. He received his PhD. from one of Europe's greatest universities, the Sorbonne, where he also taught. Faurisson told the court that the "Holocaust" is an "historical lie."

Faurisson explained that "gas chambers and the genocide together was a fraud, which led to a gigantic political and financial fraud." He cited former Israeli prime minister David Ben-Gurion's blackmailing of then West-German chancellor Konrad Adenauer into paying billions to always-broke Israel as "reparation" for "gassing" victims. To obtain the loot, Israel "committed an enormous fraud" in claiming that six million Jews were gassed, Dr. Faurisson testified.

He described the Nuremberg war crimes trials as the "witchcraft trials," saying that the confessions were extracted from fear of deportation to the Soviet gulag. The French professor compared his own experience at having been beaten by Zionist thugs on his campus, for merely daring to contradict the holy writ:

> It is not surprising that a Nazi officer would sing whatever tune his captors demanded if the alternative was having his wife and children sent to Russia. . . Many people who talk about torture don't know what it is. I know very well how people could have been under pressure. I have never worn a German uniform, I have never killed anybody yet my life is impossible. . .The lives of revisionists and their families are made unliveable by those who refuse to allow history to be questioned.

Dr. Faurisson said that the very earliest propaganda tales claimed that extermination occurred from fatal doses of steam or electricity. "I don't see why this story of electricity has been abandoned for gas. I don't see why this story of steam has been abandoned for the gas."

The professor from Vichy stated that there was not a single homicidal poison gas chamber in any Nazi concentration camp. "If it (proof of gassings) had existed, we should have thousands of material (proof). We have not one proof."

He referred to the fact that the Germans recorded everything they did in meticulous documentation. Financial records taken from the Auschwitz concentration camp list the costs for everything, even to the cost of the landscaped shrubbery and arbors. Yet there are no records of any homicidal gassings having taken place, even though millions supposedly occurred.

No more than 200,000 to 350,000 Jews died in concentration camps, Dr. Faurisson declared and these deaths were mainly from disease and privation that occurred mostly toward the end of the war, commensurate with the vicious allied bombing of German supply lines.

In discussing the figure of "six million murdered Jews," the French expert alluded to a German officer named Hoettl who just blurted this number out at his trial, with no substantiation. No one knows where he got the figure but it was made a part of the "documentary" record at Nuremberg. "This figure has just kept on being slavishly reproduced by the media and historians," Faurisson said.

At this point, Crown prosecutor Griffiths jumped to his feet and declared, "It is not the Crown's case to say that six million people were gassed." How very interesting. It is the case of the news media. But in a court of law the

GASSINGS DISPUTED

Nazi confessions false, prof claims

Nazi confessions of mass gassings of Jewish prisoners were false, a district court was told yesterday.

The statement came from a defence witness at the trial of Ernst Zundel, of Toronto, who has pleaded not guilty to knowingly publishing false information harmful to racial and social tolerance.

"The fear of being sent to Poland or to Russia" drove Nazis to confess camp atrocities at the "witchcraft trials" of Nuremberg, said University of Lyons II Prof. Robert Faurisson, 56.

"I understand perfectly why they confessed," he said.

He testified he has been beaten up frequently and hounded out of his job and many research facilities for his views as a "revisionist historian" questioning the "sacred cow" of the gas chamber genocide.

Faurisson's publications denying the wartime existence of gas chambers in the concentration camps and his conclusion that it is an "historical lie" that six

ERNST ZUNDEL
Wrongful info charges

million Jews were murdered in those camps, are sources in the two publications that landed Zundel in court.

Faurisson said, "I've killed nobody; I'm not an SS officer. But my life is impossible.

"My wife is called wife of a falsifier. My son wanted to be a judge but had to resign," he told the 10-man, two-woman jury.

"A Nazi is a man, a Jew is a man, and I am a man.

"A man says go on, confess and you will be free. You are ready to fall on your knees."

Faurisson's emotional outburst came on the morning of his third day of testimony.

He said made-up stories continue to appear. He quoted from a Jan. 21 edition of *Alberta Report* magazine.

An article entitled Eva Brewster Remembers the Death Camp purports to describe the gas chamber operation in Auschwitz concentration camp, he said.

The article, as Faurisson cited from it, says following a mass gassing, "after a few minutes, the bodies were dropped through trap doors into the crematorium."

Trapdoors, said Faurisson, are "a new detail."

The trial continues.

figure is not even defended by the lackeys of the Zionists.

Also testifying on Ernst's behalf was Dr. Russell W. Barton, senior associate psychiatrist and attending physician at Strong Memorial Hospital in Rochester, New York. In May of 1945, Dr. Barton was a medical student attached to the British Red Cross, when he entered the notorious Bergen-Belsen concentration camp.*

We are told over and over that death scenes at Bergen-Belsen were due to deliberate, "systematic" starvation of the inmates (the original "gassing" claim has been dropped for Bergen-Belsen though there have been "eyewitnesses" who swear they saw homicidal gassings there).

When Dr. Barton entered the camp he said he had been "brainwashed" to believe the worst of the Germans and to assume that the Allies were vastly morally superior to them.

However when he heard the "deliberate starvation" charge he couldn't understand it, because, if it was true, why were the camp kitchens so large and well-equipped, he wondered?

He testified that he saw considerable evidence that food supplies for all inmates, as well as hygiene, was generally good until the German army was over-run on the Eastern Front. Then internees from the German concentration camps in Poland started streaming back into Germany, where Bergen-Belsen was located, and where 50,000 were subsequently housed. Bergen-Belsen was built to house some 3,000 people. Propaganda-spouting journalists relayed reports saying the inmates had died from disease and starvation *deliberately planned and inflicted* by the Nazis, and this irresponsible rumor has been rolling like a giant snowball/ avalanche in the media ever since.

Dr. Barton said he interviewed many of Bergen-Belsen's inmates and they themselves admitted that the camp administration ran a fair operation until the over-crowding began. The Commandant was bitter over the overwhelming influx of tens of thousands of detainees from the east into his camp and felt responsible only for the original 3,000 in his care.

The camp commander of Bergen-Belsen did not try to flee the camp when the British invading forces arrived. He felt that it would be understood that he had done the best possible job under impossible conditions. "I don't think for

---

* Sooner or later revisionists will be debating the Exterminationists, many are already being interviewed on television. When Zundel debated Braden and Novak on national U.S. television they interspered the conversation with black and white photographs of thousands of dead bodies, presumably from Bergen-Belsen:

There they were: naked, starved, pathetic and genuinely heartbreaking. Bulldozers are shown pushing the bodies into mass graves. Other corpses are stacked like cord-wood in the backs of trucks. "Look at what the dirty Nazis did. How can you deny the Holocaust?," the revisionist is asked, as the righteous true believer shakes with rage. No doubt about it, this is powerful propaganda — as long as it can go unchallenged. Dr. Russell Barton poses that challenge as an eyewitness on the scene who has kept his reason and retained his original perceptions apart from the media hype.

one minute that he felt responsible for the deaths" said Dr. Barton. The commandant was hanged.

The physician added that he met many German camp personnel "who were kind and sympathetic" while the British themselves in some cases "were rather vicious."

As a psychiatrist knowledgeable of the techniques of brainwashing and psychological warfare, Dr. Barton informed the jury of the danger of mass hysteria in the media, saying that when independent judgement of right and wrong is impaired by media repetition, brainwashing occurs.

Following Dr. Barton was Thies Christophersen, an eyewitness and survivor from the usually overlooked other side. It is often forgotten that there are at least two sides to every story and that in this case, there are Germans and others who were in the camps who, despite incredible repression—Christophersen was kidnapped from Belgium by West German police for daring to testify against the Zionist hoaxers—speak out to say there were no homicidal gas chambers.

Christophersen is a 67 year old former German army lieutenant who was an agronomist stationed at Auschwitz from January to December, 1944. He testified that the air in Auschwitz was very clean. He had resided in the camp in serene surroundings in which the interned persons were treated humanely. Stories about atrocities and gassings having occurred in the camp are purely propagandistic in nature, said Christophersen.

Speaking through an interpreter, he acknowledged the existence of crematoria but said these were perfectly legitimate in a camp suffering from disease outbreaks. The former *Wehrmacht* officer related that the wife of his German commandant was cremated at Auschwitz after dying of the virulent typhus plague which haunted eastern Europe.

Christophersen is the author of a previously cited short book, *The Auschwitz Lie*, which has had a tremendous impact on the German people's awareness of the hoax that has oppressed them for these many years.

Another powerful witness for the defense was Dr. William Bryan Lindsey, a native Texan with a doctorate in chemistry from the University of Indiana at Bloomington. For 33 years he has been employed at a top U.S. corporation as a research chemist.

The chemistry whiz informed the court that the safety and time factors involved in the supposed gassing of millions of people with Zyklon B pesticide are scientifically impossible.

Said Dr. Lindsey in his historic testimony, "I have come to the conclusion that no one was willfully or purposefully killed with Zyklon B in this manner. I consider it absolutely impossible."

Not being able to wriggle out of so devastating a contradiction to the myth by so eminent a scientist, the media downplayed or suppressed it altogether. The *Toronto Sun* refused to mention that Dr. Lindsey was a doctor of chemistry, referring to him merely as a "chemist," which in a former British colony like Canada can also mean a druggist. Canada's national TV network gave absolutely no mention of Dr. Lindsey's debunking in its entire 10 p.m. broadcast.

Next to take the stand was the redoubtable Ditlieb Felderer, an anti-Zionist Jew whose family had been persecuted by the Nazis. He was born in a Nazi internment district in Austria in 1942. His family fled Nazi control by trekking over the mountains into Italy where they lived as refugees for several years after the war until their emigration to Sweden.

Felderer has conducted forensic, on-site research at the Auschwitz camp. During his 27 visits he snapped 30,000 color photographs, took soil samples and conducted infra-red analysis of rooms and buildings. He sneaked into areas off-limits to tourists and generally scoured the facility from top to bottom.

Not one of his 30,000 photographs was permitted by Judge Locke to be offered as evidence and exhibited to the jurors. His pictures of the phony Auschwitz gas chamber "vents" made of porous wood and of slapdash construction, along with wooden "gas chamber" doors that aren't even hermetically sealed as is claimed in holohoax scribblings, would have offered a powerful *visual* antidote to the lifetime of TV and movie propaganda the jurors had sat through. But it was not to be.

Felderer did testify about his discovery of giant, faked crematoria chimneys that had been put up at Auschwitz after the war by the Soviet communists, as a "symbolical" teaching. These phony crematoria chimneys didn't even have a smoke channel, Felderer discovered. He portrayed Auschwitz as it now stands as a "Hollywood set" where Zionist and communist propaganda is carried on. At the same time as faked or reconstructed exhibits have been placed on the guided Auschwitz tour (such as the infamous "execution wall" where, tourists are told, 20,000 people were executed, though Felderer could find not a single bullet hole in the wall), other areas are off-limits. In these Felderer discovered the real Zyklon B rooms the Germans had built to fumigate bedding and wearing apparel which could not readily be fumigated by steam (due to the water absorbency), and instead were fumigated by the dry method of Zyklon B.

In a rollicking exchange with the prosecutor, Felderer sarcastically lampooned the homicidal gas chamber claims and refused to be placed on the defensive. Many of his sarcastic barbs brought gales of appreciative laughter from a jury weary of the tension and sanctimony of the Exterminationists.

Felderer stood firm before an enraged prosecutor in his contention that Auschwitz was a fundamentally humane facility where inmates staged plays, performed in a male and female orchestra and danced in entertainment halls. This was more than Mr. Griffiths could endure.

"Where did you get this idea about an orchestra?" he hissed.

"From (Fania) Fenelon's book," (a book by a Jewess who was in Auschwitz entitled *Playing for Time*).

"It says nothing in there about dancing," Griffiths angrily shot back.

"Have you ever heard of a dance hall that didn't have an orchestra?" Felderer quickly answered to more courtroom laughter.

The prosecutor eventually became comically tongue-tied in the face of Felderer's rapid-fire Swiftian satire, quotes from Voltaire and bold comparison of the Zundel trial to a Soviet show trial.

At one point Griffiths tried to force Felderer to admit that he was only involved in revisionism "for the money," citing the fact that the author's book, *Anne Frank's Diary: A Hoax*, carried a $10 price tag.

"If you'll be nice to me," Felderer grinned mischievously, "I'll give it to you for free." The jury laughed appreciatively. Judge Locke and Prosecutor Griffiths scowled.

Felderer's testimony has become controversial among those who were not present in the courtroom and have to rely on newspaper accounts by journalists who, though in some ways even-handed in their coverage, mostly took offense at the witness's having poked fun at a sacred cult they themselves were only beginning to disabuse themselves of.

But to those observers whose perceptions were not clouded by Extermina-tionist piety, Felderer's testimony was seen as a tremendous benefit to the Zundel cause. Griffiths was doing everything in his power to create in the jury a sense of outrage at Felderer as the one revisionist beyond the pale. He wanted the jurors to gasp in dismay and shock, frown and become angry at the witness.

Instead, Felderer's brilliant mockery made the jury laugh. Astute observers of the ritual implications of *shoah* ("Holocaust") religiosity in our society know that satire and mockery are the elements the Exterminationists above all else cannot abide; wisely too, since any pious dogma is diminished in its mental hold on people when it is held up to public ridicule. The fact that Felderer's quick-witted repartee moved the jury to chuckle, against the obvious wishes of a frosty-faced judge and prosecutor, was a victory.

One woman-juror, who only days before had daubed at her tearful eyes dur-ing a "survivor's" testimony, was now laughing it up with Ditlieb. This was an ominous sign to the cultists.

One of the most priceless sights of the trial and one of the most eloquent testi-monies of the buffoonery of those who had insisted upon it and those who had prosecuted it, came as Griffiths waved above his head an unraveled condom that had been attached to a leaflet urging people to mail such artifacts to the fake junk pile at Auschwitz where exhibits of a similar level were housed.

"Did you mail this leaflet and the condom, Mr. Felderer?" the distraught prosecutor in the flowing black gown asked in desperate seriousness, causing the jury and some of the spectators to roar in laughter at the absurd figure he cut.

"Well, each is encouraged to send what they can," Felderer replied with a smile. Griffiths looked as if he were having a nervous breakdown.

Ditlieb offered to get him a glass of water to calm his nerves.

Other witnesses included German-Canadian parents who outlined how they and their children had been the objects of hate as a result of the endless and mendacious hoax propaganda accusing Germans of every conceivable barbarity, a hate that has been ruled out of the universe of moral concern by Establish-mentarians who refuse to acknowledge the damage done to the human rights of Germans and other European-descended people by the hoax movies.

Frank Walus took the stand, the Polish-American falsely accused of being a Nazi war criminal living in Chicago. He had been tried and convicted in the media, beaten by Zionist hoodlums and forced to spend $120,000 in legal fees (a great deal of which he still owes), to finally exonerate himself. Eleven eye-witnesses from Israel swore that Walus killed and maimed cripples and even their parents. In fact, they were all lying. Walus had been a forced laborer of the Germans during the war, working on a farm.

The Zundel defense asked Walus to appear because his ordeal demonstrated the power of the false accusers and the willingness of bigoted people to lie in order to extract revenge against a race of gentiles they despised.

Baptist minister Rev. Ron Marr, publisher of the *Christian Inquirer*, went to bat for free speech and Zundel's human rights:

> I view with the greatest gravity that any person in Canada is called to defend himself for publishing what he believes, whether it is right or wrong...(it) is suggesting that a court can come up with the truth on an (historical) issue and then that everybody should salute and say "aye sir."

Would that there were more Christian preachers unafraid to remain loyal to a Christ-like commitment to truth even in the face of vicious Zionist blackmail, blacklisting and every other type of pressure, as Rev. Marr did.

Croation-American researcher Jerome Brentar took the stand to explain how faked evidence is being used today in a witchhunt against elderly Europeans accused of "war crimes" by a controlled media and judiciary. Brentar stated that John Demjanjuk faced deportation to stand trial in Israel (surely he will get a fair hearing there), on the basis of a phony I.D. card produced by the Soviet KGB which claims Demjanjuk is "Ivan the Terrible", a cruel camp guard. When, in Demjanjuk's defense, Brentar tried to bring a Jew to the U.S. who had sworn that *he had killed Ivan the Terrible over 40 years ago*, the trip and the witness were obstructed, just as evidence at the Zundel trial relating to scale models, slides and photographs was suppressed or disallowed.

A courageous reporter (there still are a few), with over thirty years experience, Doug Collins next testified about the atmosphere of intimidation that surrounds free inquiry into the history of World War II. He said there was no topic that frightens reporters into submission to Zionist dogma more than "Holocaust" revisionism. Any newsman who investigates revisionist critiques is smeared with the "anti-Semite" label, Collins stated.

Mr. Collins warned that, should Ernst Zundel lose the case, reporters will have to check with the Jewish "Defense" League (which he called the "attack league") before having their material cleared for publication.

Since the false news law was itself Orwellian in the sense that it claimed that jurors can telepathically determine if someone "knowingly" published "false news", Collins addressed the fundamental absurdity of the verdict the jury was ordered to decide.

"Can you read this man's mind? Can you look in that man's brain and say he did or didn't know something? All you can do is look at the printed words and make a value judgement".

German historian Udo Walendy gave the jury background on the faking of photographs and the role of Zionist propagandists who were inserted into key positions in the Allied command and charged with determining what the Germans allegedly did, he too was severely restricted in what he could say and talk about by Judge Locke.

Playwright and literature professor Dr. Gary Botting of Red Deer College took the stand and informed the court that George Orwell, the great prophet who warned of the dangers of mind control, was the first to question the validity of gas chamber exterminations as far back as 1945.

Dr. Botting related an outrageous account of censorship which is almost unknown outside the province of Alberta but would be universally known if the censorship had occurred against a book of homosexual pornography or communist agit-prop.

Teaching a literature course on the "Holocaust," he was ordered to include Gerald Green's fanciful novel by that name. For balance, Botting also sought to include Dr. Arthur R. Butz's masterful refutation, *The Hoax of the 20th Century*. All 25 copies were seized by the Canadian government and pulped.

Also giving moral support to Ernst on the stand was his outstanding son, Pierre and his brave friends in the German-Canadian community.

There was only one witness left. It was now Ernst Zundel's time to defend 27 years of activism. Known as a fine speaker with a firm grasp on revisionist history, Ernst was expected to fill in any gaps in previous testimony, punch bigger holes in what had already been revealed and finish the course in triumph.

Shortly before this, and as the fortunes of the Exterminationists continued to sag, they became desperate. Their courtroom officials even began harrassing witnesses and Zundel supporters. Bullying, contempt and sheer meanness were the order of the day from some of the old guard (but by no means all of them, and the personal security many policemen gave to Ernst and his attorney after the first day of the JDL riot was undeniably professional and adequate. To those honest policemen, all Zundelists say "thank you." They know who they are).

I had film in a camera confiscated with great discourtesy by a plainclothes courthouse cop, who also happened to be a mason. Later, seated in the press gallery as the only revisionist-oriented reporter, the Zionists became disturbed about me.

Sol Littman, an unsavory individual who emanated a veritable aura of mal-evolence, attempted to have this reporter thrown out of the press gallery. As a result, I was shaken down for my press pass during a recess. Littman is not a court official but a CBC reporter. More importantly, he's the head of the Canadian branch of the Simon Wisenthal "Holocaust" Center, hence his clout. After my press pass was checked and validated, I was permitted to remain. Littman seemed a bit dismayed that I did not make any remarks to him, but I intuitively felt that this was a man who thrived on negative emotions. I chose not to satisfy his grotesque appetites. Littman, the reader will recall, was the same man who had been admonished by the judge in the preliminary hearing to refrain from passing notes to the prosecutor.

What feelings traverse a human being like Ernst Zundel when he actually confronts the greatest moment of his life thus far? One might opine that the emotion would automatically be one of elation, relief and anticipation. Yet most people only pretend to want to strive for their secret dreams and highest aspirations. Human nature being what it is, we tend to shrink from actually grasping for the steepest ledge on the tall mountain of individual destiny. Some-where inside we may sense that "going for the gold" can be frightening and treacherous—brimming with unexpected twists and unimagined last minute perils.

That's why most of us only fantasize about fulfilling our God-given destinies. We make a little show, for the sake of self-delusion, that we are striving for the most high, but we purposefully drop back just when it seems that Providence is calling our bluff.

Whether it is the set of his jaw or the angle of his ledge-like forehead or the laser-like quality of his eyes, Ernst Zundel appeared to walk to the witness box and the international spotlight of his Great Holocaust Trial, like a man who keeps appointments with destiny the way others keep dates with pretty girls.

His performance in the next several days is one of the most controversial portions of his trial. Many say he was far too candid and impractical. Still other observers point out that Ernst had one eye on the jury and exercized prudence and circumspection, but another on history and eternity, which impelled him to forego the kind of dissembling others urged on him.

When he "hit," in reply to Mr. Griffiths extremely discourteous questions, he hit like a sledgehammer. He refused to repudiate his deceased mentor, spiritual godfather and political adviser, Adrien Arcand. Arcand had founded the party of Canadian national salvation, the National Unity Party.

"He was a great Canadian," Ernst told the court with total loyalty. Did this go badly for him with the jury? Who can say? But Zundel obviously did not believe that even the greatest of victories in a courtroom would be worth a price like betraying his old friend, who had himself suffered so much, including six years imprisonment for his independent writing and lectures.

Griffiths turned to George Dietz's book *The Hitler We Loved and Why*. Ernst had provided photos for the book and his middle names had been assigned authorship, but it was largely Mr. Dietz's *opus*. Dietz had transformed the "Christof Friedrich" monniker into a kind of publishing house *non de plume* by this time.

Griffiths being possessed of the mentality of the shopkeeper and errandboy for the plutocrats that he was, gleefully pursued his singular and fallacious assertion: that Ernst was the sole author of *The Hitler We Loved and Why* and that proceeding from that "fact," Griffiths would establish that the Samisdat founder was a neo-Nazi who only *used* historical revisionism as a means for making Hitler and his politics respectable again.

This was a notion that the badly shaken press and some segments of the public *desperately needed to believe* in order to assuage their injured faith in the "Holocaust" cult which had been sustained as a result of the Christic/Zundel/Faurisson/Lindsey/Barton et al onslaught.

This need for a sustaining faith in some kind of comforting Zionist illusion and stereotype was vital to the equilibrium of an audience that had had its whole universe turned inside out in 5½ weeks of testimony. By seizing on the ADL-promoted fallacy that all revisionists secretly believe that Hitler acted out all the psycho-sexual and sadistic-pornographic Zionist fantasies projected onto this cartoon symbol of media-manufactured evil, the percipients could absolve themselves of the painful intellectual duty to confront the lies, contradictions and fabrications the revisionists had been able to shockingly expose.

Here was the master formula for the Crown: to exploit the mental flabbiness and moral capitulation of the weak-willed and easily led masses. Griffiths would hammer away at a simplistic formula: Zundel despised the colonial occupation government of West Germany and refused to acknowledge the sacred doctrine of modern society, that Hitler is the devil/anti-Christ incarnate. Therefore,

Mass Nazi gassings impossible expert witness tells Zundel trial

TORONTO (CP) — Mass gassings using hydrogen cyanide would have been physically impossible in the large, unsealed rooms that were called Nazi gas chambers, a United States chemist testified yesterday at the trial of Ernst Zundel.

William Lindsey said he can't believe historical accounts that between one million and 2.5 million were gassed at the Auschwitz-Birkenau camps in Poland.

Recognition

Lindsey was recognized by the court as an expert witness on hydrogen cyanide, the poison said to have been used to kill millions of Jews at Nazi death camps.

"After looking over the evidence ... I've been forced to conclude it is impossible for it to have happened the way it's been described," said Lindsey, a research associate at an Iowa chemical company for 33 years.

"There are too many inconsistencies.... No one was wilfully and purposefully killed with Zyklon B (gas) in this manner," added the defence witness, who said he shares "revisionist" Holocaust information with Zundel.

Zundel, 46, a West German citizen living in Toronto, has pleaded not guilty to knowingly publishing false information likely to cause social or racial intolerance.

Two of his publications dismiss Second World War genocide of Jews as a hoax and a Zionist conspiracy to extract reparations from Germany.

Zyklon B, which contains one-third liquid hydrogen cyanide, was named at the postwar Nuremberg trials as the killing agent in underground gas chambers.

Hydrogen cyanide is so deadly that 300 parts per million vaporized in air will kill humans in three minutes, Lindsey told the District Court jury.

But the underground chambers were cool, he said, and it takes a higher temperature to readily vaporize the solid Zyklon B.

Lindsey later said under cross-examination that the chemical's boiling point is 26 degrees and admitted body heat would raise the temperature in crowded chambers.

Lindsey, who visited all of the eastern European Nazi camps to pursue his interest in "allegations" of Holocaust gassings, said the chambers leaked and people outside them would have been killed.

Flimsy doors

He described the Auschwitz chamber as having two flimsy wooden doors, one with a glass pane, and a hole in the roof.

Lindsey disputed earlier testimony by a Crown witness who said he pulled wet, recently gassed corpses from the chambers.

"You can absorb hydrogen cyanide easily (through the skin)," he said. "Unless you washed quickly, you would join the alleged pile of victims you were carrying out."

One of the reasons why the Extermination theory was shaken by the trial was due to the fact that distinguished men of science were willing to risk their careers and even their lives to testify. One of these men was Dr. William Bryan Lindsey, a research scientist at a major U.S. corporation for 33 years, with a doctorate in chemistry from the University of Indiana at Bloomington. Notice that in this news report all mention of Dr. Lindsey's Ph.D. in chemistry and his work as a scientist with a major U.S. corporation has been deleted in order to lessen the impact of his testimony. He is referred to as "Lindsey" and never Dr. Lindsey. Such media tricks will not ultimately detract from the service to human enlightenment Dr. Lindsey's testimony fulfills, in exposing the superstitions of the "Holocaust" cult.

argued Griffiths, Zundel covertly knew darn well the Nazi "beasts" gassed six million Jews in "gas chambers" with wooden doors. He was only concealing the fact to rekindle Hitlerism.

The weighing of the evidence in support of the *fact* that the Nazis simply did not gas six million Jews or even one Jew, was out of consideration. The single irrational connection between a certain admiration for *some* National Socialist policies and the claim that this was ironclad proof for a belief in gassings, flew in the face of one overlooked truth.

For, one would expect that someone who *honestly* had a belief that the homicidal gassings *did not occur* (and this is all Zundel needed in order to be acquitted), would quite normally and naturally have a less prejudicial view of the Third Reich.

Ernst from early on grasped the cheap game Griffiths was playing and tried to nip it in the bud. He told the court that he is the first to freely admit that the National Socialists committed some ruthless actions in World War II. But what was to Zundel the undeniable, fundamental goodness of the Hitler party, was something he would not deny.

And there is the paradox: if he really were the sort of Machiavellian poseur and whitewasher that Griffiths claimed, Zundel would have totally disavowed Hitler and the National Socialists.

A jury of aware persons would have gleaned the honesty of his admissions without too much difficulty. It was a fact that this jury was chosen under rigged conditions and sometimes behaved that way. So Ernst would speak the truth anyway. He spoke above the profane heads of the mercenary prosecutor and the scared-rabbit jurors: he spoke to eternity. Those who say this was a bad "move" reveal themselves as part of the modern world of consumer ethics and check-book morality.

Zundel really was what he said he was—a man with a heroic dedication to the truth. He bore fidelity to the knight's code in that courtroom and left the detail of win or lose to fate and the stars.

Do I imply he was indifferent to victory or contemptuous of success? Did he bankrupt his life savings for nothing? Did he wreck his business as a futile gesture? Hardly. He is a man of many passions. He has a huge appetite for life and worldly achievement. It is the great folly of the crowd to assume that because someone operates by a knight's code that that person has an enervated or diminished zest for life. On the contrary, more than anyone in the world, Ernst wanted desperately to win acquittal. He fully grasped the implications for world peace and justice such a verdict might bring. But he would not tarnish the victory by compromising his honor. The victory would be pure, it would be holy, it would be a shining gift to the slandered and dishonored dead, to their living survivors and the unborn generations to come, or it would be whatever Divine Providence wanted it to be.

For these reasons, this was Ernst Christof Friedrich Zundel's finest hour. He set the example of the "man against time" operating as an eschatological agent on the temporal plane.

In the face of Griffith's Nazi-baiting about Dietz's *Hitler* book, Ernst spoke clearly and directly:

It's a book trying to give a different view to Hitler's Germany. He lifted the German people up by the boot straps to give them a place in the sun.

Amid the rubble of Germany's defeat, Zundel noted that he had learned what is was like to have somebody else's version of history forced on a nation of people. This "history" divided father against son and made the older people's side of the war appear to be lies and shameless deceit.

We constantly hear from the "Holocaust" propagandists that revisionism must be stopped because it could cast dreadful aspersions on the testimonies of "survivors"; therefore, out of "sensitivity" to them, revisionists should be silenced.

But the only consideration that can and must obtain in this calculus of offended feelings must be the search for the actual truth of the matter. Certainly few have cared about the devastation perpetrated against the honor and feelings of the World War II generation of German people whose own account has been denigrated and insulted for forty years, as a pack of lies.

It follows that Zundel would make the decision to commit himself to the thankless camp of the revisionists after his 1963 visit to Dachau, where he confronted a visitor's guestbook crammed with outpourings of pure hatred for the German people. It was passion, not calculation, that spurred him onward.

His goals would be nothing less than gigantic: his publishing house would serve as the groundwork for the death of Exterminationism, mercifully putting to sleep forty years of psychic trauma and incitement to murder. Next he told the court boldly, he sought to over-turn the Nuremberg kangaroo trials. After that it would be back on track for the Aryan (European-descended) people, back on their path to the stars.

If talk of Aryans and Germanity makes many libertarian and academic revisionists cringe, so be it. This is the context into which Ernst Zundel was born. From birth he was hurtled into a raging inferno, the massive holocaust that was World War II as a whole. It stamped him with its unprecedented mercilessness, injustice and wholesale waste.

If Zundel is supposed to speak and behave like a California war baby nestled cozily in a shade-tree lined Main Street of an unscathed America, if he is supposed to observe all the nuanced code-words and formal bows and scrapings of others more spoiled by an enviable life in the cocoon that was the pre-sixties U.S.A., then unreality is even more fully realized than one might imagine.

The inescapable fact cutting through the mass hallucination imposed by the all-pervasive media hoax, is that here sitting in the pressure box of the witness' well, was a true holocaust survivor. Why are his psychic lacerations not allowed to be factored into the judgement of the percipients? If he acted in a way not pleasing to all North Americans, it was because he was enamored of an Old World patrimony plugged into a stream of consciousness still in touch with the lost chord so obviously missing among many Canadians and Americans.

From this heritage he turned the tables. Genocide? What of the policies of the Jewish-American foreign policy adviser Henry Morgenthau?, Zundel asked. "That was a real, detailed plan of how to destroy Germany" he underscored.

"We Germans have long ago forgiven the world for the. . .genocidal bombing campaign of the Allies. . .and for the mistreatment of our people" he intoned to callous and pompous laughter from Zionists in the spectators section. They alone have the copyright on suffering.

Zundel held firm, outlining the "first declaration of global war on Germany" made in 1933 by declaration of the American Jewish Congress, which launched a world-wide boycott.

"The effect on the German government was near panic," Zundel declared. Having seriously destabilized the government, the war pledge "certainly explains (that) there were two protagonists that preceded the struggle in World War II. If there were hard feelings by Germans against Jews it was as a direct result of this propaganda," he revealed.

"That explains some of the anti-Jewish measures taken by the Nazis," Zundel stated. The organized Zionists launched their economic war solely because they refused to countenance a Germany for the German people, ruled by the "Blood and Soil" committment of an indigenous yeoman peasantry. This right to rule a nation's destiny was reserved solely for the coming state of Israel. For Germany to wish for the same thing for its own folk was a grounds for war.

Griffiths suggested that Zundel's "fixation" on Jews implied that they were a problem. Zundel rebutted:

> There are race problems, there are Jewish problems. (CTV reporter) Brian Nelson was fired for touching on the Jewish problem. He called Israel "the Zionist entity" (in a TV broadcast from Kuwait), and was kicked out of his job. That was the Jewish problem for Nelson.

Zundel's diamond-like logic was the Samisdat problem for prosecutor Griffiths.

Trying desperately to paint the 46 year old dissident as a violent, phony pacifist, Griffiths cited the sale of souvenir "combat buckles" (a Samisdat fund-raiser which has been very lucrative for the Jews who traffic in Nazi paraphern-alia in a multi-million dollar a year industry but off-limits to Germans like Zundel). Also cited was Ernst's former call for "gun barrel justice" for traitorous Germans who cooperated in the communist torture and terror against tens of thousands of German civilians. Zundel foresaw fair trials (fairer than he or Arcand ever received) and then execution, if guilty. He could oppose war and war-mongering as a pacifist without renouncing capital punishment. Later, he explained his motivation for penning *The West, War and Islam*, the jeremiad for which he was also in the dock.

> It might sound grandiose, but I thought I could defuse a very dangerous situation. Like many writers and publishers, I thought I had something unique to say. I wanted to defuse a situation in which we were drifting toward war in the Middle East.

Attempting to be as humble as he could in the face of a badgering, fascist-baiting bully like Griffiths, Ernst related how he had pleaded forthrightly with former Ontario provincial Attorney General Roy McMurty, the Zionist puppet who was muttering about locking up peddlers of "hate literature," to provide Zundel with guidelines for avoiding the problematic phrases. In 1983, Zundel informed the court that he had written McMurty pointing out that the Attorney General's failure thus far to supply the necessary information concerning McMurty's definition of a thought crime, constituted entrapment.

As usual in his quest for dialogue and open communication he was completely rebuffed. Zundel had told McMurty, "I see no reason why you would be embarrassed to supply guidelines to hate literature to the general public. It would be cheaper than prosecuting an innocent person who transgressed the law." But recently the Canadian government had been profligate in squandering the taxpayers money on the pet whims of the Zionist lobby. The Great Holocaust Trial cost the Canadian people hundreds of thousands of dollars. Perhaps more.

Zundel's testimony on everything from the doctored content of the Anne Frank Diary to the essential accuracy of the book for which he was being tried, *Did Six Million Really Die?* (which he admitted contained a few honest errors, but was fundamentally not as flawed as the books authored by witnesses the Crown produced to try and convict him), are packed with important facts and details outside the scope of this writing.

But one of the many gems we can lift pertains to the all-important motivation of the "Holocaust" hoaxers.

"Why would anybody go through such an elaborate ruse?," revisionists are often asked. We reply in terms of the reparations paid to Israel (100 billion marks) or the diversionary tactic of taking notice away from Israeli genocide as well as providing the fundamental *raison d'etre* for the very existence of the Zionist state.

Zundel's personal research exposed a heretofore unknown factor. He quoted in court from a Feb. 29, 1944 letter from H. Hewett, assistant secretary for the British Ministry of Information which states the need to divert attention away from the war crimes and atrocities of the Soviet Red Army. Ernst's research point on this matter centered on the letter which was accepted as an exhibit in the trial. It reads:

> . . . We cannot reform the Bolsheviks but we can do our best to save them — and ourselves — from the consequences of their acts. The disclosures (of Soviet genocide) of the past quarter century will render more denials unconvincing. The only alternative to denial is to distract public attention from the whole subject. Experience has shown that the best distraction is atrocity propaganda directed against the enemy . . . your cooperation is therefore earnestly sought to distract public attention from the doings of the Red Army by your whole-hearted support of various charges against the Germans and Japanese which have been and will be put into circulation by the Ministry. (Cf. *Allied Wartime Diplomacy* by Edward Rozed).

Zundel followed this stunning piece of evidence of the manufactured nature of the Extermination myth with the point that all that was needed to get the Big Lie rolling was the concept of Victor's justice and morality — winners absolved of all crimes, losers go on trial. From this the word of the Allies became dogma and later became the holy writ of newspaper and TV "truth," as a result almost solely of endless repetition in public.

In response to this four decade-old continuation of wartime propaganda that should have died with the war, the Samisdat publisher told the jury that dissidents like him must be allowed to sound "the alarm bells and expose unpopular facts" in the quest for a world without war.

Shortly thereafter Ernst left the witness box to return to his center court-room enclosure in the defendant's seat. The marathon trial was coming to a close. Adrenalin pumped into the veins of partisans on both sides. The fate of more than a book was at stake. Doug Christie wasted no time in his summation, in outlining the stakes:

> There are a lot of people who would like to see their enemies right there (prisoner's box). If we start down that road there will be no stopping those politicians who want to put their opponents right there. And don't think they can't find the power. There are pressure groups today who have the power—just ask him (Zundel). . . For the sake of freedom I ask you never to forget what is at stake here. The accused stands in the place of anyone who desires to speak their mind. Even if you don't agree with him, you must take it as a sacred responsibility not to allow the suppression of someone's honest belief.

It was five hours of impassioned homily—from crescendo to crescendo as Mr. Christie shouted his fiery conviction on behalf of truthseekers and free-thinkers, to the ceiling of the York County courtroom. He thundered and he whispered. He cajoled and he demanded.

He called it the most important trial in Canadian history:

> You 12 people have more power in your hands for good or evil than any 12 people I ever met. When you are finished with your delibera-tions, in all probability this country will never be quite the same. A clear answer of the innocence of my client will put an end to a process that could lead to the destruction of all society.

Facing off directly against the issue of Extermination, fact or fantasy, Christie told the jury:

> If my client chooses not to believe it, give him that right. The accused has a right not to believe it. If you want to believe it, fine. All we ask is that the accused be given the right not to believe it.

It appeared, at that time, that the defense attorney had indeed swayed the jury and that Griffith's epithet-ridden, *ad hominem* counter-summation did little or nothing to overturn Christie's dramatic defense of free speech.

Stomping all over the Charter of Rights, Griffiths acknowledged that Christie's address to the jury had been "stirring and passionate" (just as he would later grudgingly admit that the defense was extremely well-prepared and

Samisdat's publisher in the prisoner's dock.

THE JURY

"You twelve people have more power in your hands for good or evil than any twelve people I ever met. When you are finished with your deliberations, in all probability this country will never be quite the same."—Douglas Christie, in his summation.

"Canada will be the same no matter which way you rule."—Judge Locke, in his final instructions.

schooled), but he said, free speech was beside the point, because freedom of speech was just a "red herring."

That was certainly true for the Canadian government which would apparently shatter any custom of fair play and sportsmanship to please its elite masters.

Judge Hugh Locke also addressed the jury with his usual feigned reasonableness and patronizing. Casting all impartiality to the wind, he directly attacked one of Doug Christie's best points: that this was a landmark case among landmark cases which would indeed alter the entire fabric of Canadian society.

"Canada will be the same no matter which way you rule," Locke lied to the jury. He also at this time took unofficial "judicial notice" of the gas chamber extermination claim.

Judicial notice is usually used in a court exclusively for establishing universally recognized verities over which any arguing would merely constitute absurd time-wasting. For example, judicial notice is taken of the fact that the sun rises in the east, and so forth.

But in a break with precedent in 1981, a California judge, Thomas Johnson, had taken judicial notice of the crazed and contrived gas chambering in the preliminary hearing involving the Institute for Historical Review (IHR) revisionist organization and the lawsuit of survivor-industry operative Mel Mermelstein, making the outcome for the IHR one of almost certain fore-ordained defeat.

Judge Locke did not take the formal notice which the American judge had. Such notice would have forbidden a presentation by the defense of revisionist evidence and arguments. One can only state that a providence of some kind must have interceded and restrained Locke in this matter. In every other matter pertaining to the defense he came on like Telford Taylor or any other judicial bully.

Locke's informal "notice" consisted of telling the jury that he himself believed in the overwhelming "truth of the Holocaust." He cited the screening of the Hollywood director's war-time propaganda film showing healthy-looking German camp personnel contrasted with anorexic prisoners as "proof" that the Germans were not also victims in the way Jews were. A more fatuous or mediocre comment cannot be imagined. The man, despite his aristocratic airs, was, at bottom, just a boob-tube booby, incapable of envisioning a reality beyond the Hollywood scene flat.

Because Allied propagandist George Stevens chose not to show his audience Dresden, Hamburg or any other German city of any size mercilessly incinerated in an authentic holocaust in every sense of the word, Locke surmised that it didn't happen.

It is this reporter's opinion that prior to Locke's instruction to the jury, a vote for acquital or at least a hung jury was a distinct possibility. But consider the element of Locke's cleverly biased and loaded instruction: The County court judge now himself implied what the verdict must be: The gassings happened, exactly the way the Zionists said it did, inferred Locke, and with all the dotted i's and crossed t's of the British Ministry of Information directive on the subject. What stolid Canadian man-in-the-street could buck this?

Locke *could* have said that it was a fascinating trial where many startling turnarounds were witnessed, and left it, impartially, at that. He didn't. He denied reality as much as any Rudolf Vrba or Raul Hilberg.

With the JDL threatening from one side and the judge giving the verdict from the other, the jurors had little room to maneuver. They retired on the 28th of February. Shortly after their opening deliberation they asked for the entire trial transcript. Apparently there were some grounds for questions and further discussion among them. Locke refused them their request, offering the summation speeches of the attorneys instead.

The jury retired again and on March 1st, 1985 returned a verdict of not guilty to a charge of wilfully promoting false news with regard to the essay *The West, War and Islam*. The essay had declared that Zionists were greedy, vicious and militant, created the "lie of the Holocaust" to blackmail Germany into bankrolling the building of Israel and were conspiring with bankers, communists and Freemasons to establish a one-world slave society.

I like to think that this verdict is a trade-off or compromise between one or more jurors who were profoundly affected by the case offered by the defense on the one hand, and the other bored, apathetic and indolent jurors who simply wanted to do their "duty" to the Zionist god and get back to consuming. Surely the acquittal on so serious and powerfully indicting a writing, is an important victory for Ernst.

Unfortunately, on the second count regarding *Did Six Million Really Die?* they decided on guilty.

They celebrated anyway, Ernst and the boys, with Zundel hoisted on the shoulders of his best friends and giving the victory sign.

Some say this was merely a clever pose that Ernst, the ever-savy media showman, struck for the front pages of the world's newspapers.

But perhaps Ernst Zundel saw something far-away as he rode those shoulders, maybe he saw the cheering multitudes of future generations.

III

AFTERMATH

I think it was a much messier affair than we expected it to be in terms of things coming out we didn't want.

Ellen Kachuck, B'nai B'rith of Toronto
(*Globe and Mail* 2-28-85).

. . . in the long run he won the propaganda war hands down . . . Coverage of the court case gave Zundel and his cronies more ink, more attention, more platforms from which to shout than can be purchased with all the money in Conrad Black's bank account.

Walter Stewart, Columnist, *Toronto Sun*
(Black is one of the wealthiest men in Canada)

Jews are not — and never were — in any danger of ethnic gas chambers or Siberian exile in North America. The only possible danger they face . . . is the one they themselves may well create: the anti-Semitism that could arise from their zealous prosecution of . . . Ernst Zundel . . . their unrelenting demands that forty years or forever after the war (unlike the relatives of the other many millions of victims) that anyone who allegedly killed one of theirs must be brought to justice, even if he has to be kidnapped, and the exercize of their undoubted political clout to prevent other citizens of a free country from reading books they have every right to read.

Les Brewley, Columnist, *Vancouver Sun*

On March 25 Judge Hugh Locke sentenced Ernst Zundel to 15 months in prison and 3 years probation. Hence forward he is under a judicial gag order forbidding him from writing or speaking about the hoax. After spending a night in jail, Ernst was released on $1,000 bail. In late spring he was ordered deported to West Germany whenever he finishes serving his prison sentence.

Doug Christie is appealing the conviction and Zundel says he will take it to Canada's highest court. The grounds for appeal are fertile indeed. But what effect politics will have on the appeal-judges is not difficult to guess. The appeal will center on the Canadian Charter of Rights, the rigged nature of jury selection and the suppression of photographic evidence.

As a result of his conviction, he joins a distinguished fraternity of writers and publishers. Voltaire languished in the Bastille for six months for a satire on the French regent. Galileo was under house arrest for years for having overturned Church dogma. Solzhenitsyn went to the gulag for opposing Canada's Stalinist ally.

Griffiths and Locke meanwhile join the ranks of Torquemada et. al. as the instruments of state despotism.

The newsmen who covered the trial with a measure of impartiality are under fire from Jewish pressure groups. At a special Orwellian conference "investigating" these reporters at the conclusion of the Great Holocaust Trial, the journalists were warned about their "anti-Semitism" (being fair to the opponents of Zionism is construed as "race hate" by these megalomaniacs).

Manuel Prutschi of the Canadian Jewish Congress vented his outrage over a Zundel trial headline published in the *Globe and Mail* which read "Lawyer Challenges Crematoria Theory." This was the previously-cited reference to defense attorney Doug Christie's presentation of technical facts which showed that a crematorium does not give off smoke and flame, as "Holocaust" folklore repeatedly claims. Prutschi told representatives of the newspaper that there must be no further headlines of this sort, because the headline "implied that the Holocaust is not a documented fact."

The reaction of the Zionist-controlled media to the trial itself is a highly recommended and fascinating study for all who wish to observe a second media hoax in action.

First, the Newspeak word "Holocaust" was employed to maximum effectiveness. Pictures of crematoria ovens with skeletons inside them, piles of emaciated bodies at the concentration camps and scenes of SS guards roughing up partisans were widely published. "How could the Zundel crackpots deny this undeniable 'Holocaust'?" they very cleverly asked.

But what is the definition of this ambiguous and universally used word of "holocaust?" What specifically does it denote?

In a strict and proper sense the word is supposed to refer to the deliberate extermination of six million Jews by gas chamber poisoning, mainly.

Do crematoria, piles of bodies and excesses by some soldiers prove this fantastic "Holocaust" claim? Not at all.

Here is where linguistic manipulation enters in and this is why the word "Holocaust" came into currency all of a sudden in the media from 1967 onward.

By grouping things that did happen and that Zundel and revisionists never denied in court: that there were crematoria, that possibly hundreds of thousands

On the day of sentencing, Zundel carried a cross to the courthouse. Shortly after, Judge Hugh Locke sentenced him to 15 months in prison.

Holocaust scholar quoted 'madman,' publishing trial told

By KIRK MAKIN

One of the world's leading authorities on the Holocaust has quoted selectively and extensively a German SS officer who was obviously a madman, the defence at the Ernst Zundel trial has alleged.

Among the claims sworn to by the Nazi, who ultimately hanged himself while awaiting trial for war crimes, was a statement that 25 million Jews were killed in two small extermination camps and that 700 to 800 people could be crammed into a 25 square-metre gas chamber.

"Don't you think it reflects on an author that some statements are absolutely ridiculous?" defence counsel Douglas Christie asked Raul Hilberg, a professor at the University of Vermont who has spent more than 35 years studying the Holocaust.

Mr. Zundel is charged with two counts of publishing false news which caused or was likely to cause racial or social intolerance. His articles question the Holocaust and postulate an international conspiracy of Communists, Zionists, bankers and secret societies. The Crown must prove Mr. Zundel knew the information was false.

Prof. Hilberg agreed that Obersturmbanfuehrer Kurt Gerstein, the SS officer, was most unreliable on some topics covered in some affidavits. But Prof. Hilberg defended his decision to quote the officer on other subjects in a book he wrote on the Holocaust.

Obersturmbanfuehrer Gerstein was one of the few people who could provide information about gas chambers at the the Treblinka and Belzec camps in Poland, Prof. Hilberg explained.

The officer said he was responsible for dispensing poison to several camps in Poland to be used to kill internees.

"Beyond that, I realized, of course, what kind of person he was and I did not rely on any statements I regarded as imaginative or incredible," the witness said. "I think he was given to great excitability. What can you say?"

Prof. Hilberg can quote selectively with impunity, then his client is not guilty of any sin either.

For most of the morning session, Mr. Christie and the witness engaged in a grim battle over what really took place during the last days of the Warsaw ghetto uprising and whether documents exist to show Adolf Hitler actually ordered the extermination of the Jews.

Prof. Hilberg said nobody has to believe or try to verify there was such an order just because he concludes in this book that there was.

Mr. Christie then asked if that statement could not also apply to the articles Mr. Zundel is charged with publishing.

"No, it is not the same," Prof. Hilberg said.

The argument was typical of the strenuous going-over Prof. Hilberg's writings and previous testimony are getting at the hands of Mr. Christie. The lawyer demands precise sources for everything and then frequently criticizes those.

One protracted argument concerned the use of the word "resettle" in Nazi reports and whether it was a euphemism for annihilate, as Prof. Hilberg fiercely maintained.

"The word used was relocate," Mr. Christie said at one point. "To me, that doesn't mean annihilate."

"That's the difference between you and me," the witness replied hotly. "I've read thousands of documents. I know what it means in the context."

"You alone understand, right?" Mr. Christie asked sarcastically.

Later, Mr. Christie questioned whether crematoria Prof. Hilberg saw on a recent trip to Poland were really as the Germans left them.

"They were as you've been told the Germans left them, right?" he asked.

"I was not present when these buildings were blown up," Prof. Hilberg said in exasperation.

"You could say he was crazy," Mr. Christie said crisply. The lawyer accused Prof. Hilberg of quoting only those statements from the "madman" which bolstered conventional ideas on the Holocaust.

"I'm not making diagnoses here," Prof. Hilberg replied. "I would not characterize him as totally rational, but I'm not here making those kind of judgments."

Prof. Hilberg has been accepted as an expert witness. He has testified that about five million Jews were exterminated by the Nazis.

Yesterday, he said some of the SS officer's claims were outrageous, while others, such as the number of people who could fit into a chamber, warranted skepticism.

He said it was intellectually sound to use the portions which withstood scrutiny or seemed plausible, while making no mention of the outlandish statements. "For my purposes, it sufficed that there were gas chambers," he said.

Mr. Christie maintained that if

Articles such as this one, while scrupulously accurate, enraged "Holocaust" cultists who, after the trial, held a special inquisition denouncing reporters for being "used" by the revisionists. Accustomed to the media's obsequious affirmation of every "Holocaust" tale, however distorted or exaggerated, the Zionist lobby was unprepared for the kind of questions posed by Zundel's attorney and revisionist team of researchers. Believing their own press notices, the Exterminationists predicted a walkover. When the testimony did not go according to the preconceived script, reporters were scapegoated for deviating from it. Fortunately, Hilberg's logic-chopping is a matter of the court record: The esteemed "expert" revealed that he did not inform his readers of the parts of Gerstein's "confession" which he concealed. Such a "scholar" continues to exert his authority only due to the glamor heaped upon him by the Zionist-dominated media, who, since the trial, have consigned Hilberg's unprecedented admissions to Orwell's "memory hole."

of Jews died from typhus disease and unintentional starvation brought on by merciless Allied bombing of supply lines, and placing them all under the heading of "Holocaust," *people are led to believe that this is what is being denied.*

This is the delerious confusion inherent in the Newspeak linguistics which George Orwell warned against in *1984* (see his appendix). It is this confusion that is exploited to maximum effect by the Exterminationist propagandists. They want people to believe that revisionists are saying that there were never any concentration camps, no crematoria, no deportations, no innocents killed.

But no revisionist from Butz to Berg to Faurisson to Martin has ever held this. It is the caricature of the Exterminationists about the revisionists. Why do they need to invent this lie about revisionism? Let us examine the cover story of Canada's equivalent of *Time* magazine, the important and nationally circulated *Maclean's* magazine for March 11, 1985. It is devoted to the Great Holocaust Trial.

If the "truth" was vindicated by that trial and gas chambering proven, why would *Maclean's* have to lie about the trial or distort the testimony? Wouldn't it be damaging enough just to accurately report it as it happened, if all went as well for Zionist orthodoxy as the Establishment now claims?

In reporting Arnold Friedman's testimony, the magazine says that doubt was cast on it when the witness was forced to admit that flames were not coming out of crematoria chimneys. What reason does *Maclean's* cite for this doubt having been cast?

Intriguingly, like the *Boston Globe, Chicago Tribune* and *NY Times,* *Maclean's* does not mention the scientific fact that crematoria cannot give off these flames and odors by virtue of the very patent of the builder's technical specifications.

Why would *Maclean's* be reluctant to mention this? It was *the exact basis for the admission that came from Mr. Friedman. Maclean's* omits this vital evidence and instead substitutes a secondary point of Mr. Christie's, that there were factory chimneys in the area that could have emitted smells and smoke too.

Why didn't *Maclean's* mention Mr. Friedman's sworn testimony about seeing color-coded flames according to which nationality of Jew was being "burned?" If a revisionist had said something as kooky as that it would have been a banner headline in *Maclean's.* Why protect Friedman from the results of his own hallucinatory statements?

In reporting the testimony of Raul Hilberg, the magazine neglected to mention the "minor point" that Hilberg had confessed that there was no scientific proof that even one Jew was gassed. Why is that going down the memory hole? Why does it have to be evaded? Is there something about this fact that makes the fatcats at *Maclean's* so nervous they have to hide it? Why? One would think the "Holocaust" claims were overwhelmingly true and easily proved, so why the need to conceal such newsworthy data as the leading "Holocaust" historian admitting that there is no scientific proof of any Jews having been gassed?

Maclean's article made no mention of the fact that Hilberg admitted to editing Gerstein's purported confession without informing his readers that he did so. No such damaging revelation like this was elicited from Dr. Faurisson or any of the other revisionist witnesses, and if it had been we can be well

Disease killed Nazis' prisoners, MD says

By Wendy Darroch Toronto Star

Thousands of prisoners who died at the Bergen Belsen concentration camp during World War II weren't deliberately starved to death but died from a rash of diseases, according to a psychiatrist who was there in 1945.

Russell William Barton, 61, of Rochester, N.Y., said that when he entered the camp on May 2, 1945, he had heard and believed that prisoners were deliberately starved to death by the Nazis.

But Barton, who was a medical student volunteer with the British Red Cross, said if that was true, he couldn't understand why the camp kitchens were so well equipped.

He told a District Court jury yesterday he decided the stories of vicious German inhumanity weren't true after he found books, dating back to 1942, itemizing the amount of food cooked and distributed each day.

The psychiatrist was the second defence witness at the trial of Ernst Zundel, who has pleaded not guilty to two counts of publishing statements he knew were false and likely to incite mischief.

The publications in question are *Did Six Million Really Die?* which claims the Nazis had no gas chambers and Adolf Hitler never plotted to exterminate the Jews, and *The West, War And Islam,* which contends Zionists, Freemasons, communists and bankers are conspiring to form a world power.

In his pamphlet *Did Six Million Really Die?* Zundel, a 46-year-old Carlton St. publisher, has reprinted part of an article written by Barton. He states that Barton's recollection of camp conditions is "a surprisingly honest appraisal of the situation at Belsen in 1945."

Barton, senior associate psychiatrist and attending physician at Strong Memorial Hospital, said the appalling conditions of the camp were likely due to massive overcrowding and the camp administrator's resentment because 50,000 prisoners were kept in a camp for 3,000.

The camp administrator felt it was his responsibility to look after the 3,000 prisoners, not the 50,000 who had arrived after the Russian front began to push west, the doctor said.

Barton said that when he first approached the camp he could smell decaying corpses and feces.

He and another student were assigned to a wooden hut where 400 people were lying on the floor, some of them dead, others with feces and vomit smeared on their faces, some trying to reach for help, the jury was told.

"I was stunned," the doctor said.

The prisoners were suffering from malnutrition, gastro-interi-

tis, typhus, scurvy and a multitude of other diseases, he recalled.

He said that, when he tried to give prisoners protein intravenously, some of them screamed, saying others had died from injections administered by the Germans.

Intravenous injections were new to medicine at the time, Barton said, and the deaths were likely caused by bad reactions to them.

Another defence witness, French professor Robert Faurisson, said the "gas chambers and the genocide together was a fraud which led to a gigantic political and financial fraud."

Israel's former prime minister, David Ben Gurion, had twisted the arm of former West German chancellor Konrad Adenauer in order to obtain reparations payments for the relatives of dead and missing Jews, Faurisson said.

To get those payments, "Ben Gurion committed an enormous fraud" in saying 6 million Jews were murdered, Faurisson said.

Barton

The evolution of the canonical "Holocaust" story is not as unambiguous as gospel is supposed to be and true believers wish. The vintage tales, circa 1945–1960, told of poison gas extermination in concentration camps located in Germany proper like Dachau, Buchenwald and Bergen-Belsen. When those camps had to be dropped from the list of gas chamber facilities due to the revelations of even pro-Zionist historians such as Martin Broszat (and the gassing accounts "moved" east to the camps in Poland), a new yarn was concocted: the internees at places like Bergen-Belsen were the victims of inten-tional starvation as the method of extermination. By cleverly exploiting to maximum value the emotional content of photographs of piles of corpses in such camps, this fundamentally fallacious assumption has gained nearly total acceptance in the public mind. Dr. Russell William Barton is not only an authority on brainwashing but as a medical student he accompanied the British Red Cross into Bergen-Belsen in 1945. His crucial testimony reveals the facts behind the "Holocaust" gospel's myth: conditions in German camps deteriorated commensurate with the loss of the war. Starvation was not deliberate. Dr. Barton's courageous account of his eyewitness experience—while reported during the trial, as above—has been blacked out of subsequent accounts in the aftermath of Zundel's conviction. It constitutes testimony extremely subversive of the enshrined dogma about German concentration camps and rather than being squarely faced, examined and debated, is suppressed and ignored.

certain it would have been mentioned prominently and with plenty of tittering in *Maclean's*.

Hilberg's admitted fraud is dropped from the Establishment record the Big Brother publishers wish to fabricate concering the trial. They are fairly good at it too, having had decades of practice in fabricating the history of World War II by the same omissions, suppressions and distortions.

Writes Canada's supposedly "prestigious" national weekly magazine: "But equally vigorous cross-examination by the defence attorney could not alter the testimony of Holocaust survivor Rudolf Vrba."

That damnable lie is from p. 43 of the issue cited. "Could not alter his testimony"? What do they call his confession that he never really saw any gassings? What do they call his having claimed at the very last minute, after a lifetime of saying otherwise, that his book is not factual, not a "document for a court" but "an artistic rendering" based on hearsay?

Will *Maclean's* be sued for false news for this lie they feel compelled to push in order to prop up a man like Vrba?

But more importantly, again the question is, why is *Maclean's* so insecure that they would have to lie about what Vrba admitted in court? Could it be that the top manipulators know very well that the homicidal gas chamber accusations are indeed a hoax? Why else would they so blatantly doctor the account of the trial?

The reader should note how *Maclean's* is counting on the laziness and gullibility of its readers. They are banking on the gamble that their readers will not check the transcript of the trial themselves, and that they haven't even saved or remembered the newspaper clippings of the Totonto press which covered Vrba's testimony and even headlined his confession of never actually having seen gassings himself.

The media has a very low opinion of their reader's intelligence.

Maclean's also completely left out of its story of the trial any mention of the crucial scientific testimony of corporate research chemist Dr. William Bryan Lindsey. Dr. Lindsey testified that the gas chamber tale as stated is impossible. *Maclean's* completely suppressed any mention of Dr. Russell William Barton who was in Bergen-Belsen concentration camp and talked to the inmates who told him conditions were good until overcrowding brought on by Germany's impending military defeat occurred.

Here we see the crack in the media's front of omniscience. They can't deal with the testimony of Drs. Lindsey and Barton and they can't afford to report what Hilberg and Vrba and Friedman actually confessed and why. The "Holocaust" hoax has only existed for this length of time based on these very methods of censorship, omission and outright lying.

Journalists truly confident in their beliefs would not have to resort to lying in order to make the Canadian people believe that the trial was a victory over tinpot, flat-earther revisionists.

The journalists don't have enough confidence in their own beliefs to report the trial completely and accurately and this is their Achilles heel. Taking a cue from Zundel's maxim to "know your enemy" and "exploit his weakness," we can devastate these media manipulators and this cultic priestesthood masquerading as "Holocaust historians," whenever we can organize the public

Witness indecisive

Lawyer challenges crematoria theory

SATURDAY, JANUARY 12, 1985

By KIRK MAKIN

Ernst Zundel's lawyer challenged the testimony of a Holocaust survivor yesterday, telling the man he couldn't have seen concentration camp chimneys belch smoke and flames from exterminated Jews because crematoria don't emit anything.

"I suggest it is quite impossible for smoke to come from a crematoria from human beings," said Douglas Christie, whose client is charged with spreading false news. "What do you say about that, sir?"

"Nothing," Arnold Friedman, prisoner number B14515, initially replied. "If you're talking of crematoria in Toronto and crematoria in Auschwitz, those are two different things. In Birkenau (part of Auschwitz complex), smoke came out of the chimney."

"I put it to you that you don't really understand anything about crematoria, to say: 'Aha, that is a crematorium', because that is quite wrong, sir," Mr. Christie said.

Many observers in the packed courtroom were left shaking their heads or fidgeting uncomfortably as Mr. Friedman, 56, then agreed that perhaps Jews were not being burnt in the chimneyed buildings.

Over a two-day span, Mr. Friedman has testified repeatedly to seeing thousands of boys herded toward the crematoria, and of seeing trainloads of people unloaded near the ominous buildings.

He told of how he and the other young boys in the camp had heard terrified screams and seen the flames climb higher and smoke billow anew shortly after new trainloads arrived.

Mr. Friedman said the young

TESTIMONY — Page 2

FRONT PAGE

Testimony

From Page One

challenged

internees even thought they could tell whether fat or skinny people, Ukrainians or Poles, were being cremated by looking at the color of the smoke.

Mr. Friedman's sudden indecision in the face of Mr. Christie's forceful questioning touched off an almost-perceptible shockwave in the courtroom. "Couldn't there have been many other explanations (for the smoke and flames)?" Mr. Christie asked, pressing home his advantage.

"Yes, there could have," Mr. Friedman replied. "If I had listened to you at the time when I was listening to other people (in the camp), I might have listened to you. But at the time I listened to them."

The dramatic testimony took place at the trial of Ernst Zundel, who has pleaded not guilty to two charges of knowingly publishing false news which caused or was likely to cause damage to social and racial tolerance.

In one of the two articles forming the subject of the charges, the author maintains information on the Holocaust has been grossly exaggerated or faked. One of the Crown's tasks is to prove Mr. Zundel knew the articles were false.

The crematoria theory challenged by Douglas Christie is clearly stated in the second paragraph of this article: "I suggest it is quite impossible for smoke to come from a crematoria from human beings." For Douglas Martin and the *New York Times* however, such a challenge could not be accurately and fairly reported since the *Times* and most other U.S. Establishment media outlets routinely feature scientifically impossible fables about billowing smoke emitted by Nazi crematoria. To inform their readers that the latest "Holocaust" movie or "survivor" book depicting "smoking furnaces" is so much hokum and has been for forty years, would obviously not endear the media to their readers. Hence, Douglas Martin, in a p. 2 article in the February 15, 1985 issue of the *Times* "reinterpreted" this report in favor of the carefully cultivated media image of revisionists as insane kooks. Wrote Martin, "The upshot has been a bizarre flurry of newspaper headlines calling the existence of crematoriums in Nazi death camps a theory not a fact . . ." By suppressing Christie's authentic objection and claiming that he was actually denying that cremation facilities existed in German camps, Martin superbly serves the cause of fabrication of the documentary record. The public's right to know is not very well served by such tactics, but how important is that right in light of Zionist priorities?

BOOK 'AN ARTISTIC PICTURE'

Survivor never saw actual gassing deaths

By DICK CHAPMAN
Staff Writer

A concentration camp survivor yesterday admitted he never witnessed anybody being gassed to death and his book about Auschwitz-Birkenau is only "an artistic picture . . . not a document for a court."

Rudolf Vrba, now an assistant professor at the University of B.C., told the Ernst Zundel trial that his written and pictorial descriptions of the Auschwitz crematoria and gas chambers are based on "what I heard it might look like."

Zundel is charged with knowingly publishing false information about the Holocaust that harmed or was likely to harm racial or social tolerance.

ERNST ZUNDEL
False information charge

Defence attorney Doug Christie, of Victoria, B.C., challenged Vrba's earlier testimony that he saw a Nazi SS soldier in a gasmask pouring poison gas into a low bunker connected to a Birkenau crematorium.

Vrba admitted yesterday he was never inside that particular bunker, after Christie suggested it was the roof of a mortuary Vrba had seen, not a gas chamber.

Vrba also admitted some of the thousands of women, elderly and children he claimed were marched directly to gas chambers upon arrival might have been going to the camp's bathhouse.

"Yes. Some of them actually went there (bathhouse) and more went to the gas chambers," said Vrba, who claimed many babies were gassed to death.

Vrba said his 1944 drawings of the Auschwitz camp layout were inexact and Christie suggested Vrba didn't even know exactly where the bathhouse was located.

Christie said new arrivals had to march between two crematoria to get to the bathhouse, but Vrba insisted the area ended in a "closed road" and "nobody ever came out of there except smoke."

Vrba, who escaped the camp in Poland in 1944 with a mission to warn one million Hungarian Jews of their impending slaughter, insisted he'd made accurate ("within 10%") estimates of 1,765,000 mass-murder victims up to that point.

He said some narrative passages in his book *I Cannot Forgive* are based on accounts from others.

One Vrba account says it took 90 minutes to burn a corpse, another said it took 20 minutes.

"I also include things I heard from reliable sources," Vrba said, explaining the changes in his later report.

Vrba's 1961 affadavit quotes a Nuremburg War Crimes Trial document as relating to Auschwitz gas chambers and claims it backs up Vrba's account.

When Christie pointed out that ("Nazi government") documents say nothing about gas chambers, Vrba replied: "It might be a typing error."

Vrba, whose book states the total Auschwitz death toll was 2.5 million, testified Holocaust historians Raul Hilberg and Gerald Rietlinger were limited by "historical discipline" when they made lower estimates — 1 million and about 850,000 respectively — and did not have the benefit of Vrba's eyewitness experiences.

Vrba also said increasing estimates of the Auschwitz death toll in the decades after World War II "just shows that better scholars with better methods are constantly improving the information."

He defended "errors in good faith" in his 1944 Auschwitz accounts, which he made two weeks after escaping, as due to "great urgency" to warn Jews.

The Toronto Sun, **January 24, 1985**

According to the March 11, 1985 issue of *Maclean's,* **Canada's equivalent of** *Newsweek,* **this testimony never occurred:** *"But equally vigorous cross-examination by the defense attorney could not alter the testimony of Holocaust survivor Rudolf Vrba."* **This is the theological component of "Holocaust" cult psychology in action. If reality does not conform to the dogma that "survivors" are never wrong, never exaggerate and never contradict their "eyewitness" claims, then reality must be denied and soothing myths of infallibility substituted.**

sufficiently to demand a debate and an accounting.

As I look over the figurative ton of press clippings from the aftermath of the trial, I detect a tone of desperation in the loud protestations of how wrong Zundel is. I note how often reliance on the clever confusions involved in the employment of "Holocaust" Newspeak are spouted. I observe what they avoid, what unpleasant testimony they skirt, what profoundly destabilizing contradictions they skip over. "By their evasions, ye shall know them," methinks.

It is just what they seek to avoid and censor that we can be sure are the facts they cannot answer or explain away.

I must have read two dozen mocking newspaper accounts of Ditlieb Felderer's claim that Auschwitz concentration camp had a swimming pool for the interned. "How dare he utter this evil lie which dishonors my dead relatives!", the cultists scream. Does it matter to them that there really was this swimming pool, that the *Globe and Mail* published the first picture of it ever to appear in a newspaper in the world in its March 1st 1985 edition? The same picture an insecure Judge Locke ruled inadmissable as evidence? This picture of the Auschwitz swimming pool which clearly shows that it was located *inside the fence* (i.e. for use by the internees) at Auschwitz?

No, the *actual fact* of the Auschwitz swimming pool is discounted and ignored for the sake of the *theological belief* that there couldn't have been a swimming pool in Auschwitz. That is cultism, pure and simple. Here is bias and ignorance on the part of people who have made careers out of pontificating against these vices.

Crown prosecutor Peter Griffiths unknowingly revealed the magical and mystical nature of this folklore hidden under a massive media conspiracy. Rebuking Doug Christie for not showing proper reverence for the "Holocaust survivors" (though defense witness Thies Christophersen, a survivor of the Allied mass murder/firebombing holocaust at Dresden was shown no special consideration from Mr. Griffiths), the prosecutor used an interesting phrase:

"I'm surprised he (Christie) felt it necessary to attack the integrity of people who *miraculously survived* (the gas chambers)." (My emphasis).

Yes, Mr. Griffiths, there does seem to be a strong element of the "miraculous" in the "Holocaust" tales. It would have to be a *miracle* for millions to survive what the Zionists say was the "methodical" and "meticulous" Nazi extermination program. Yes, Mr. Griffiths *it would take a miracle* for smoke and flame and ash and odors to have come out of the Auschwitz crematoria the way the inmates say that it did.

It would take a *miracle* for the wooden doors and lids on the Auschwitz "gas chambers" to have kept the Zyklon B inside without escaping to gas the guards and clean-up people as well. And so it goes.

This element of the irrational has been very little considered by revisionist researchers. The "Holocaust" hoax is maintained by Newspeak linguistics and the cult psychology employed by any irrational sect. It's just that this particular sect is dressed up in a particularly dazzling rainment of media and academic prestige which few of even our brightest minds can see beyond.

It only takes some common horse sense to sort this controversy out. It's something the common folk used to have in abundance before they abandoned themselves to the "modern world" and the pop mythology of TV soap operas

Scientific evidence of Holocaust missing

TORONTO (CP) — No scientific reports prove Jews were exterminated in Nazi gas chambers, a Holocaust scholar conceded Thursday at the trial of Ernst Zundel.

But numerous historical documents show that Jews were killed during the Second World War, said Raul Hilberg, a University of Vermont political science professor.

And even though German war documents contain no mention of killing Jews, euphemisms for death, such as 'resettlement' and 'special treatment' were used so commonly that Heinrich Himmler, head of the Gestapo, requested substitute phrases, Hilberg added.

Hilberg, who has spent 36 years studying the Holocaust and the subsequent Nuremberg trials of war criminals, testified earlier for the Crown that five million Jews were killed during the war.

Zundel, 46, a West German citizen living in Toronto, is charged with two counts of publishing statements that are

known to be false and likely to cause injury or mischief to the public interest of maintaining special and racial tolerance.

Two of his publications — one called Did Six Million Really Die? — postulate that the Holocaust was a hoax to vilify Germans and exact compensation payments from them.

"Can you give me one scientific report that shows the existence of gas chambers anywhere in Nazi-occupied territory?" defence counsel Douglas Christie asked Hilberg in a day-long rapid fire of cross-examination.

"I am at a loss," Hilberg replied.

"You are (at a loss) because you can't," Christie said.

The witness countered that there are aerial photographs of concentration camps, examples of ruined or reconstructed gas chambers, German industrial documents describing the lethal nature of various gases and filters for gas masks were found at the camps.

Hilberg agreed with Christie there are no autopsy reports in-

dicating even a single person died from exposure to poisonous gas in chambers.

He has uncovered, however, a man, took extensive notes from written request by a German scientist for some human subjects he wanted to kill by gassing in order to cut off their heads for anatomical research.

"In tens of thousands of (Nazi) documents, people were 'resettled' or 'the Jewish problem was solved' but the word killing was used only for dogs, not in reference to annihilation of Jews," Hilberg said.

Hilberg quoted from his book The Destruction of European Jews a message to Himmler from a Nazi official named Greiser stating that the "special treatment" of 100,000 Jews at a concentration camp would be complete in two to three months. Greiser then asked permission to have 35,000 tubercular Poles transferred to the camp for special treatment so they wouldn't infect Germans.

When Christie questioned Hilberg's interpretation of the last request, an exasperated Hilberg

replied: "This was not a hospital.".

Zundel, a balding, heavy-set man, took extensive notes from the prisoner's box during the day.

Hilberg told the district court jury of eight men and two women that Zundel's published account of some details of the Nuremberg war trials, which lasted from 1946 to 1949, was "fanciful."

His exhaustive research has not uncovered any evidence to support Zundel's supposition that Nazi officials were tortured to exact untrue statements implicating German war criminals, he said.

Christie introduced numerous accounts by German officers and a report by two American judges sent to investigate allegations of torture of German prisoners to back Zundel's claim that in one case, 139 prisoners were flogged until they bled and their genitals were trampled

Despite Hilberg's disinformation about "aerial photographs, examples of ruined or *reconstructed* gas chambers" (my emphasis) and talk of gas masks (which were obviously necessary for fumigation) he could not recoup the damage done by his historic admissions. Like the witch-cult which could produce only confessions and "eyewitnesses" to prove congress with the devil, Exterminationist theologian Hilberg relies on similar "proof" for his conspiracy theory about the Nazis. Scientific, forensic evidence is completely absent. But through the cinematic magic of Hollywood, such

evidence is not necessary for making believers out of millions of people. Admissions such as Hilberg made here would seriously damage the credibility of almost any historian in another field. But Exterminationist historians are carefully shielded from criticism by the media monopoly. When Hilberg's new edition of his book *The Destruction of European Jews* was reissued later in 1985, newspapers such as the *New York Times* lauded it. No mention of Hilberg's highly newsworthy revelation at the Zundel inquisition was made of course, by the *Times*.

This is the swimming pool that the Zundel defence claims visitors to former Auschwitz camp are not allowed to see. The photo was taken by Ditlieb Felderer, a Swedish Holocaust revisionist who was a defence witness.

The *Globe and Mail*, March 1, 1985

The nationally circulated *Globe and Mail* published this photograph for the first time anywhere in the world. The notion of a swimming pool for inmates at Auschwitz was denounced by the prosecutor and forbidden from being entered as an exhibit by Judge Locke. Felderer took 30,000 photographs in the course of 27 extensive trips to Auschwitz. None were allowed as evidence. Exterminationist "expert" Raul Hilberg had never even been to Auschwitz until 1979, although he wrote the "definitive" college textbook on the subject in 1961.

and a two minute capsule of the latest CBS World "news."

It took a Swabian peasant from the Black Forest of Germany to see through the incredible glamor and coverup and to shout that the "emperor" is as naked as a jaybird.

Those modernists who think Zundel is finished have no idea of the elements involved here. The Great Holocaust Trial will be the springboard for some great feats of truth campaigning.

Throughout this writing I have tried to show how Zundel's "judo" took the energy directed against him and used it to his advantage. Every time. Again and again. In every trial.

To Sabina Citron and all the others, we owe a debt of gratitude. They gave him, this time, an incredible amount of energy. I think that by the time the revisionist rocket is finished charging up on it, it is going to shake the West to its foundations.

"A lie is never young but once" wrote Chesterton, and the lid is off the biggest lie, not just of the 20th century but of our entire historical experience.

Wrapped deeply inside all of the media lies about this trial is the truth. It exists in the transcript. It is unsullied. It gleams with the fire of an entire nation of people who have been the scapegoat for the crimes of an entire age. To preserve this truth in purity and fire Ernst Zundel may lose 15 months of his life. He may be deported. He may have to endure great suffering. But the truth will remain and it will grow.

It was Ernst who did what others thought could never be accomplished: he has dealt a fatal blow to Exterminationism.

The signs are all around us. In Canada in early May, I saw that Zundel was still in the papers every day—on the front page and in the editorial comments. The Establishment simply cannot exorcize the ghost of suppressed facts brought out in that trial.

The Zionists are more hysterical than ever in trying to fight these facts by the usual Hollywood means: spectacles, marches, proclamations, movies, stories, denunciations and diversions.

The more their desperation rises, the more they re-cycle the ludicrous, world-wide "ghosthunt" for the witchdoctor Mengele—while the Soviet who designed bombs disguised as children's toys which have maimed thousands of Afghan kids, walks free; while the Israeli jet bombers of schools and hospitals sip their cocktails on their verandas in Haifa—the more they indict themselves.

Even modern people have a limit to the amount of mind-pollution, hypocrisy and brainwashing they will tolerate, especially now that they are aware of the increasingly puzzling hysteria over a four decade old war in which the propaganda actually increases with time rather diminishes. They also have a troubling itch in their intellects, a seed of healthy doubt and long suppressed skepticism reverberating from what they have heard about the trial.

Reversing the Nuremberg trials? Overturning the gas chamber hoax? These are not Zundel's only goals. It is to reassert the destiny of the people of Europe cruelly sidetracked by a lie so immense—that is Ernst's ultimate goal.

He will continue to assist the movement for renaissance for our people for years to come. He remains a symbol of this movement to restore balance on the planet.

If the Zionists continue to sidetrack the destiny of nations, to proclaim nationalism and self-pride only for Israel while denying it to Europe and North America, our planet is headed for more earth-rape, more war and even a Third World War in the Middle East.

The movement of Walter Darré in the 1930's died a premature death. Many sense it was crushed out before it even had a chance to really take root. It remains a path for the greening of the West and the restoration of the natural plan for this entire planet, in the face of the insanely artificial world that is being built up all around us.

The best way to honor Ernst for the heroic assault he has led which has helped sow the seeds of future victory, is to emulate his example.

We can begin to sense the tradition he represents. It is for us to honor that tradition. There is more to this battle than facts and numbers. The cycle of heaven is changing, and God-given forces are extending their hands to us.

If Ernst Zundel has seen a little farther or acted with more insight than many of us, it is because he knew enough to stand on the shoulders of giants. We have the ability and the duty to do the same.

One of those giants is still on earth, in Spandau-Berlin. All the newsprint, all the shimmer and glow of the consumer hell-on-earth, all the lies of the media stacked end-on-end and girdling the globe, are not the equal of this lone man. He is a light unto these dark, inhuman times.

"I have an idol in my life" Ernst told the reporters on the day he was convicted, "he is Rudolf Hess. As long as he is alive you won't see me shed a tear or bat an eyelash."

WORLD WAR TWO REVISIONISTS

MICHAEL A. HOFFMAN'S EIGHT HOUR DOCUMENTARY TELEVISION SERIES ON BETA AND VHS VIDEOCASSETTES.

Part One: Ditlieb Felderer. A comprehensive two hour interview with pioneering revisionist researcher Felderer, author of *Anne Frank's Diary a Hoax* and *Auschwitz Exit.* He discusses the diary, his discoveries of faked exhibits at Auschwitz, his imprisonment in Sweden and his view of racial and religious identity as manipulated by Zionism. VT-2, $49.00.

Part Two: Hans von der Heide. While still a teenager, von der Heide served in a combat unit of the 10th Panzer Division of the Waffen SS. With moving sincerity and clarity he recounts his fighting experiences on the Eastern and Western Fronts, Allied war crimes in Belgium and Ukraine, his ordeal as a POW and the struggle of the SS veterans today against falsification of their record. 70 minutes. VT-3, $49.00

Part Three: Tour of Auschwitz Fakes (videotaped slide show). After his landmark books, Ditlieb Felderer is best known for his edifying slide shows. In the course of 27 visits to Auschwitz, he took 30,000 photographs revealing phoney crematoria chimneys, crudely chiseled "poison gas vents," flimsy wooden doors supposedly hermetically sealing the "gas chambers" and other absurd, Hollywood-level fakes promoted to tourists as "Nazi artifacts." 2 hours. VT-4, $49.00

Part Four: Dr. Robert Faurisson. An in-depth, two hour interview with Robert Faurisson, Ph.D., The Sorbonne, Professor of Text and Document Criticism at the University of Lyon and the foremost European revisionist. VT-5, $49.00.

Part Five: Thies Christophersen. German agronomist Thies Christophersen was stationed at Auschwitz concentration camp from January to December of 1944. Through an English-language interpreter, he refutes the wildly exaggerated tales of smoking furnaces and death-dealing gas chambers. Christophersen also relates his experience as a witness to an authentic holocaust—the merciless and deliberate Allied incineration of the people of Dreden. 22 minutes. VT-6, $39.00

Part Six: Eric Thomson. This is an excellent lecture on Exterminationist mythology by the chief of research and archives for Canada's Samisdat Press. Thomson received his BA from the University of California at Berkeley and Master's degrees in Political Science and International Relations from San Francisco State. Mr. Thomson is a former instructor with the U.S. Information Agency. 30 minutes. VT-10, $49.00

(All times approximate)

MIKE GUSTAV'S
THE GREAT HOLOCAUST TRIAL
A ONE HOUR TV NEWS DOCUMENTARY
ON BETA AND VHS VIDEOCASSETTE.

This professionally produced program takes the viewer from the preliminary hearings in December of 1983 through the shocking, Winter, 1985 spectacle itself.

You'll meet Dr. Robert Faurisson, Dr. William Bryan Lindsey, Dr. Russell Barton, Prof. Gary Botting, Frank Walus, Thies Christophersen, Douglas Christie, and of course, the defendant himself in top form debating, questioning and extemporizing from his publishing house headquarters, on the street and in the courtroom. Viewers will also confront the popes of Exterminationism—Hilberg, Friedman, Vrba and Citron. In addition to the courtroom drama, extensive footage of the harrowing mob-riot and fight scenes are displayed in all their ferocity as Ernst's buddies valiantly protect him and his legal defense team from beatings and even assassination. There is never a dull moment in this fast-paced, jump-cut edited documentary by filmmaker Mike Gustav. VT-7, $49.00.

Save $34. Order all seven videocassettes for only $299.00
When ordering please indicate which format (BETA or VHS) you desire.

Order from:
The Institute for Historical Review
P.O. Box 1306, Torrance, CA. 90505
Calif. residents please add 6½% sales tax.